CHILDREN WITH DISABILITIES: A LONGITUDINAL STUDY OF CHILD DEVELOPMENT AND PARENT WELL-BEING

Penny Hauser-Cram
Marji Erickson Warfield
Jack P. Shonkoff
Marty Wyngaarden Krauss

IN COLLABORATION WITH
Aline Sayer
Carole Christofk Upshur

WITH COMMENTARY BY
Robert M. Hodapp

Willis F. Overton
Series Editor

MONOGRAPHS OF THE SOCIETY FOR RESEARCH IN CHILD DEVELOPMENT
Serial No. 266, Vol. 66, No. 3, 2001

1-02

#48167752

 BLACKWELL
Publishers   *Boston, Massachusetts   Oxford, United Kingdom*

CHILDREN WITH DISABILITIES: A LONGITUDINAL STUDY OF CHILD DEVELOPMENT AND PARENT WELL-BEING

CONTENTS

COMMENTARY

ABSTRACT

HAUSER-CRAM, PENNY; WARFIELD, MARJI ERICKSON; SHONKOFF, JACK P.; and KRAUSS, MARTY WYNGAARDEN. Children with Disabilities: A Longitudinal Study of Child Development and Parent Well-being. *Monographs of the Society for Research in Child Development*, 2001, **66** (3, Serial No. 266).

This *Monograph* presents the results of the Early Intervention Collaborative Study, a longitudinal investigation of the cognitive and adaptive behavior development of children with developmental disabilities and the adaptation of their parents, extending from infancy through middle childhood. The study was designed to generate and test conceptual models of child and family development and contribute to the knowledge base that informs social policy and practice.

The sample for the investigation reported here consists of 183 children with Down syndrome, motor impairment, developmental delay and their families who were recruited at the time of their enrollment in an early intervention program in Massachusetts or New Hampshire. Data were collected at five time points between entry to early intervention and the child's 10th birthday. Home visits were conducted at each time point and included child assessments, maternal interview, and questionnaires completed independently by both parents.

Trajectories in children's development and parental well-being were analyzed using hierarchical linear modeling. Predictor variables were measured at age 3 years when children were exiting early intervention programs. Children's type of disability predicted trajectories of development in cognition, social skills, and daily living skills. Children's type of disability also predicted changes in maternal (but not paternal) child-related and parent-related stress. Beyond type of disability, child self-regulatory processes (notably behavior problems and mastery motivation) and one aspect of the family climate (notably mother-child interaction) were key predictors of change in both child outcomes and parent well-being. A different aspect of the family climate—family relations—also predicted change in child social skills. Parent assets, measured as social support and problem-focused coping, predicted change in maternal and paternal parent-related stress respectively.

The implications of these findings for both the science of child development and the policies and practices of developmental intervention are discussed.

I. INTRODUCTION

The development of children with disabilities and the adaptation of their families present an array of challenges to researchers, policymakers, practitioners, and parents. For some, the diverse developmental pathways followed by children with disabilities provide important opportunities to expand our knowledge about human variation. For others, the diagnosis of an impairment calls for the formulation of an intervention strategy to promote more positive outcomes. Central to both is the need for greater understanding of how children with disabilities and their families change over time, and why some do better than others. The Early Intervention Collaborative Study (EICS) was initiated in 1985 to address these complex and compelling issues.

The EICS is an ongoing, nonexperimental, longitudinal investigation designed originally to address three interrelated goals: (a) to analyze individual differences in the development of children with disabilities and in the adaptation of their families over time, (b) to generate related conceptual models of child and family development that integrate research on children with and without special needs, and (c) to contribute to the knowledge base that informs social policy and the delivery of intervention services. From its onset, the design of the study has been guided by models of human development that are ecological, contextual, and transactional (Bronfenbrenner, 1979; Lerner, 1996; Sameroff & Chandler, 1975) and by an interest in the concepts of vulnerability and resilience (Rutter, 2000; Werner, 2000).

The first phase of the investigation, which was described in a previous *SRCD Monograph* (Shonkoff, Hauser-Cram, Krauss, & Upshur, 1992), focused on the development of 190 infants and their parents during their initial year of participation in a community-based early intervention program. The findings presented in this second *Monograph* were generated from the continuing sample of 183 participants who were assessed at five points in time, from their entry into an early intervention program during the infant or toddler years through the child's 10th birthday. This

1

investigation represents the largest and longest running study of children with a range of developmental disabilities and their parents ever undertaken in the United States. The richness and the longitudinal nature of these data provide a wealth of opportunities to analyze the interactive nature of child and family adaptation and, most important, to study developmental change over time.

The findings presented in this *Monograph* can be used to inform both theory and practice. In the process of bridging these two domains, the study builds on two complementary historical contexts and addresses two converging agendas for the future.

TWO HISTORICAL CONTEXTS

From a historical perspective, the EICS is embedded in two related contexts. The first rests on decades of research in child development, which can be characterized as a continuous evolutionary process. The second is reflected in decades of social and political action on behalf of persons with disabilities, which can be viewed as a dramatic revolutionary transformation.

The history of child development research is rich and multidisciplinary. In the first half of the 20th century, competing theorists staked out opposing positions on the nature-nurture spectrum (e.g., Gesell 1925; Skinner, 1953; Watson, 1928), and empirical investigators cataloged the sequential emergence of discrete skills (e.g., Binet & Simon, 1916; Gesell 1925). In the latter half of the century, scholars shifted their focus to the transactional impacts of biological predisposition and environmental influence, and emphasized the extent to which all human development occurs within a multilevel ecological context (Bronfenbrenner, 1979; Lerner, 1996; Sameroff & Fiese, 2000). At the outset of the 21st century, dramatic advances in molecular biology (including the decoding of the human genome) and the emergence of increasingly sophisticated methodologies in the developmental and social sciences are generating a more refined understanding of the inextricable interaction between biology and experience (National Research Council and Institute of Medicine, 2000). Concurrently, research interest has shifted from a predominant focus on concrete skills and "normative" behavior to a more balanced interest in underlying developmental processes (e.g., self-regulation and executive functions) and individual variation, both within and across population groups.

Within this evolving context, the explosion of developmental research (particularly in the neurosciences) has augmented the public's appetite for scientifically driven guidance to enhance the competence of *all* children—from the healthy youngster whose parents are seeking the key

2

to competitive advantage, to the child with severe disabilities whose family is searching for an intervention strategy to "unlock" the child's potential for more adaptive functioning. Central to each perspective are the over-arching questions of how constitutional predisposition and environmental factors influence the establishment of developmental pathways early in life, and how individual trajectories can be modified over time.

In contrast to the more gradual evolution of knowledge about child development, the social history of developmental disability in the United States over the past 50 years is truly one of revolutionary transformation. Caldwell (1973) summarized the major features of this revolution in her identification of three major historical periods. The first, which she la-beled "Forget and Hide," was characterized by the virtual invisibility of persons with significant disabilities as a result of institutionalization or sequestered family care with minimal public support. The second phase, which extended over the 1950s and 1960s, was called "Screen and Segre-gate." During this period, children with disabilities were evaluated and labeled, but their care was provided in specialized settings that main-tained their isolation from mainstream experiences. The third phase, which began in the 1970s, was labeled "Identify and Help." Expressed most dra-matically in the letter and the spirit of The Education for All Handi-capped Children Act (Public Law 94-142), this period was marked by a determination to provide publicly supported evaluation, education, and related services to promote more normalized life experiences. Recently, this has been augmented by a more expansive approach to full social inclusion (both within the schools and throughout society) and by a grow-ing emphasis on empowering families and building parent-professional partnerships (Meisels & Shonkoff, 2000).

This continuing social and political revolution has generated a grow-ing demand for valid and reliable information about the strengths and needs of children with disabilities and their families. Concurrently, increas-ing research interest in the phenomenon of individual differences has highlighted the potential learning opportunities offered by studies of chil-dren with atypical developmental patterns associated with a range of spe-cific impairments. This convergence of policy and scholarly concerns underscores the need for greater attention in mainstream child develop-ment research to the developmental trajectories of children with special needs. The EICS addresses this traditionally neglected need.

TWO CONTEMPORARY AGENDAS

In looking toward the future, the findings presented in this *Monograph* address two important challenges facing the field of child development.

3

The first resides in the domain of science. The second relates to the world of policy and practice.

The science of child development at the dawn of the 21st century is poised at an unprecedented threshold. On a conceptual level, there is now abundant evidence to indicate that the longstanding debate regarding nature versus nurture is not only fruitless but is fundamentally misguided (National Research Council and Institute of Medicine, 2000). The biological and social-cultural split that has been so evident in the past is now being reconceptualized as developmentalists are constructing more complex relational models (Overton, 1998). Thus, both social scientists and molecular biologists currently agree that the process of human development is guided by a dynamic and mutual interaction between both nature and nurture. That is, genetic expression is moderated by environmental influences and the developmental impacts of experience are moderated by constitutional characteristics. One consequence of this conclusion is that the continued compartmentalization of research on children with biologically based disabilities makes very little sense.

Much of the existing knowledge base about "normative" child development has been generated by studies of white, middle-class children who are free of identified biological impairments. Thus, the inclusion of children with diagnosed disabilities into the mainstream of child development research presents a previously underappreciated opportunity to enrich both the construction of theoretical models and the design of empirical investigations that could be conducted to test and refine them. Stated simply, the formulation of normative developmental theory has been constricted by the extent to which it has paid little attention to children who have been classified as "abnormal." This traditional exclusion is problematic, not only because it contributes to an insidious form of discrimination, but also because it results in a skewed and incomplete science. This investigation seeks to redress this shortcoming, particularly in its focus on underlying developmental processes, especially self-regulatory behaviors, as potential predictors and moderators of differential change, rather than on the simple measurement of standardized cognitive outcomes.

Beyond its contributions to developmental theory, we address several critical issues currently facing the domains of policy and practice for children with disabilities and their families. Three challenges are particularly worthy of mention. First is the need to establish appropriate and attainable longer term goals for children with a wide variety of disabilities that vary in both their nature and their level of severity. This is particularly important in view of the extent to which children display a wide range of skills, not necessarily predicted by chronological age. Second is the need for more precise identification of the predictors and moderators of developmental change that are amenable to intervention. This is especially

4

important to facilitate more targeted intervention strategies and the continuous refinement of service models over time.

Third is the need for reliable and valid empirical data to guide the differential allocation of programmatic resources to support the development of vulnerable children and the adaptation of their families. Central to this challenge is the recognition that formal services add value as a supplement (not a substitute) for a family's own adaptive capacities and resources. Thus, in an equitable system, not everyone would or should receive the same services. In contrast, differential resource allocation should be guided by an assessment of the extent to which each family (and its own informal support system) is able to meet its children's needs adequately, followed by the identification of those whose difficulties require additional services and supports. To this end, the ability to analyze how child and family characteristics at age 3 years (at the time of termination of early intervention services) predict the shape and rate of change in child development and parental adaptation over the early and middle childhood years provides a promising vehicle for anticipating differential service demands during the full span of the childhood period.

In summary, the findings we present have important implications for both the science of child development and the policies and practices of developmental intervention through the early and middle childhood years. As such, they underscore the need for greater intellectual cross-fertilization among researchers, policymakers, practitioners, and parents in their collective search for both greater understanding of the development of children with disabilities and more effective strategies to enhance their prospects for productive and fulfilling lives (Shonkoff, 2000).

II. THE DEVELOPMENT OF CHILDREN WITH DISABILITIES AND THE ADAPTATION OF THEIR PARENTS: THEORETICAL PERSPECTIVES AND EMPIRICAL EVIDENCE

In this chapter we examine the literature on the development of children with developmental disabilities and the adaptation of their parents to these disabilities. Much of the literature on both topics is descriptive and cross-sectional, rather than theoretically based and longitudinal. Efforts to understand sources of variability in child development and parental adaptations are increasing, however, and are often rooted in applications of theories of child or family development constructed originally for general populations.

In this regard, important work on children with disabilities and their parents has emerged from the growing field of developmental psychopathology, which addresses issues of both prevention and intervention (Overton & Horowitz, 1991). This field has been guided by two interrelated principles: (a) an understanding of the causes and organization of both adaptive and maladaptive behavior can be gained through the application of developmental theory and (b) knowledge of the extent to which developmental processes are universal requires the study of atypical populations (Luthar, Burack, Cicchetti, & Weisz, 1997). Much of this research has focused on understanding the development of maladaptive behavior in populations with psychological dysfunction (Sroufe & Rutter, 1984). This approach to understanding normative development and its deviations is particularly valuable to those who study individuals with mental retardation and developmental disabilities.

Zigler's (1967, 1969) seminal work on children with mental retardation demonstrated the advantages of a developmental approach and served as a stimulus for the application of a developmental perspective to a broad spectrum of individuals and behaviors. Although no single theory defines the focus of research emerging from the field of developmental psychopathology, much of this work has been guided by either organismic approaches (e.g., Beeghly & Cicchetti, 1987) or an ecological/transactional model (e.g., Sameroff & Fiese, 2000). These frameworks represent different explanatory models, but are similar in their use of the organic system as the central metaphor (Overton & Horowitz, 1991) and their roots in system theory in positing that development is constructive, organized, and integrated. Thus, a systems approach to understanding the development of those with mental retardation and other developmental disabilities guides much contemporary work.

This chapter begins with a brief review of longitudinal studies of the development of children with developmental disabilities and then examines the literature on two potential agents of developmental change—the child's instigative efforts and parental/family factors. We then consider the literature on family and parent adaptation to having a child with a developmental disability, and examine the relation of specific characteristics and developmental processes of the child as well as of other parental/familial resources to the well-being of the parents.

LONGITUDINAL STUDIES OF CHILDREN WITH DEVELOPMENTAL DISABILITIES

Longitudinal studies offer multiple benefits to the field of child development because they can provide critical perspectives on the pathways of development and on intra-individual differences in those pathways. Such studies uncover processes, examine stability and change in specific domains of functioning, and identify predictors of change in developmental trajectories (Lerner, Hauser-Cram, & Miller, 1998).

Although few in number, the majority of longitudinal studies of children with developmental disabilities have three characteristics: They concentrate on one aspect of development (e.g., cognitive development), focus on one group of children (e.g., children with Down syndrome), and are of limited duration (generally, the first few years of life) (e.g., Dameron, 1963; Dicks-Mireaux, 1972; Reed, Pueschel, Schnell, & Cronk, 1980). Further, the studies are primarily descriptive and track change in children's cognitive level over the infant and toddler period. As a whole, these studies have resulted in a similar pattern of findings—that although the cognitive level of children with Down syndrome may be relatively high during infancy (i.e., in the 70–80 standard score range), by 3 years of age such scores are consistently in the low-to-moderate (i.e., 40–50) range. This does not imply that these children are losing skills, but that they are not making gains at the same rate as typically developing children. Language development has been noted as an area of particular weakness for children with Down syndrome (Gunn & Crombie, 1996), and cognitive assessment batteries are heavily language based after the infant years. Therefore, some of the decline noted in standard scores may be due to their increased emphasis on language.

Three longitudinal studies have unique features that distinguish them from most research in this area. Carr's (1988, 1995) London study of children with Down syndrome is noteworthy because she followed children from 6 weeks to 21 years of age, yielding data covering the longest period of any such study. The findings for the development of cognition demonstrate a decline in standardized IQ scores from infancy (average 70–80) to 11 years (average 30–40) and then stability through age 21. Carr reported high correlations between intelligence scores at ages 11 and 21 ($r = .9$), but emphasized that some individuals (17% of the sample) showed changes in IQ of more than 10 points over the decade of study. Therefore, although ordinal position tended to remain stable, some individuals made large changes in cognitive skills, the majority in a downward direction.

The investigation by Sigman and Ruskin (1999) is unique in its comparison of the competencies of children with autism, Down syndrome, and developmental delay. They focused on the relation between children's early skills in interpersonal communication and symbolic representation and their later social competence during middle childhood. Although Sigman and Ruskin reported that concurrent associations among nonverbal communication, play, and language were similar for all three groups, they found that children with autism displayed early deficits in the processes of joint attention. In contrast, children with Down syndrome displayed deficits in expressive language as well as declines in scores on intelligence tests from early to middle childhood, but their nonverbal skills, prosocial skills, and play skills were relatively strong. Children with developmental delay were similar to children with Down syndrome although they did not show similar strengths in representational play skills or weaknesses in expressive language skills. This study is valuable for its delineation of distinctive patterns of deficit of children with different biologically based disabilities.

In a short-term early childhood longitudinal investigation, Beeghly and Cicchetti (1987) studied 41 children with Down syndrome (ages 20–76 months) over a 1-year period. Despite the short time frame, their study is distinctive in its theoretical grounding in the organismic-developmental perspective of Werner and Kaplan (1963), which posits that development unfolds within an organization of interrelated systems and becomes increasingly differentiated and hierarchical. Werner had, in fact, studied children with mental retardation in developing this principle and had noted the importance of distinguishing the psychological *processes* involved in behavioral change from the behavior itself (Werner & Strauss, 1939). Beeghly and Cicchetti (1987) reported that children with Down syndrome were more delayed in expressive language than in other domains of symbolic functioning (such as symbolic play) but that their representational abilities were organized in ways similar to their typically developing peers. They found an organized and coherent but slower (than typical for the chronological age) pattern of development in the social-communication system, and that children with Down syndrome became increasingly autonomous and more cognizant of their own symbolic activities over time, as would be predicted from organismic-developmental theory.

Though organismic-developmental theory is rich for its potential application of developmental principles to understanding the child's developing symbolic cognitive systems, ecological theories posit aspects of children's characteristics and contexts that can be tested as predictors of development. Developmental-contextual theory (Lerner, 1991, 1996), in particular, offers a perspective that places the child within interrelated and interacting systems in which patterns of changing relations occur (Overton, 1998). From this perspective, development is viewed as relatively plastic, and the child is considered to be simultaneously an agent in constructing his or her own development and a respondent, influenced by the multiple systems in which he or she participates (Brandtstädter, 1998). Specifically, the family system is known to exert a powerful influence during the early years of life (Minuchin, 1988). In the following sections we review the literature on children with developmental disabilities as agents of their own development and on the relation between the family context and children's development.

CHILDREN WITH DISABILITIES AS AGENTS OF THEIR OWN DEVELOPMENT

Many interacting systems guide a child's emerging competencies, but children also act as agents in constructing their own development (Overton, 1997), though they vary in the extent that they are able to alter its course. Children with developmental disabilities are more constrained by physical and cognitive limitations, yet we would expect that, like other children, they also function as agents in the enhancement of their abilities. Self-regulatory processes are particularly central to self-agency (Bruner, 1996). Children who are able to regulate their behavior, both when engaged in intellectual challenges and when confronted with frustrating or demanding situations, show developmental advantages over those with poorer self-regulation (Bronson, 2000). Empirical support for the importance of two features of self-regulation, the motivation to master challenging tasks and self-control of emotions and behavior, are discussed in the following sections.

The idea that the impetus to learn is an intrinsic aspect of human behavior (Ryan & Deci, 2000) has long been a central principle of constructivist developmental theories (e.g., Piaget, 1952). Robert White (1959) maintained that as children come to perceive their actions as producing effects on the environment, they develop a sense of efficacy, accompanied by feelings of pleasure. He further proposed that this sense of efficacy leads to an iterative series of transactions between the child and the environment that result in increasingly competent behavior.

Harter (1978, 1981) proposed a model of effectance motivation that expanded on White's thesis. According to this model, early experiences with success and positive feedback from caregivers result in an internalized system of self-rewards, standards, and goals, and children become increasingly less reliant on positive feedback from caregivers as their internalized systems develop. Some children, however, maintain an extrinsic motivation orientation due to frequent failure and/or dependence on others.

Mastery motivation, one aspect of effectance motivation, relates to children's attempts at object-related mastery. During the toddler and preschool years, children attempt to master problem-posing tasks. As defined by Morgan, Harmon, and Maslin-Cole (1990) mastery motivation is "a psychological force that stimulates an individual to attempt independently, in a focused and persistent manner, to solve a problem or master a skill or task which is at least moderately challenging for him or her" (p. 319). Researchers have emphasized two aspects of this definition. First, the child needs to attempt to complete the task independently, without suggestions or other forms of scaffolding from others. Second, the task needs to be sufficiently (but not overly) challenging to the child, as motivation is greatest on tasks that are just beyond the child's current level of skill (Harter, 1974).

The results of several studies indicate that higher levels of mastery motivation measured during the infant and toddler period predict higher levels of cognitive performance during the subsequent 1 to 2 years (e.g., Jennings, Yarrow, & Martin, 1984; Yarrow et al., 1983). Importantly, evidence from studies of children with cognitive delays or mental retardation report that they appear to be as persistent on challenging tasks as other children with similar mental age during the infant and toddler period (e.g., Hauser-Cram, 1996; MacTurk, Vietze, McCarthy, McQuiston, & Yarrow, 1985; Ruskin, Mundy, Kasari, & Sigman, 1994). Thus, both developmental theory and empirical evidence suggest that learning to persist in the face of challenge guides the participation of young children with developmental disabilities in their own cognitive growth as it does other children.

Behavior Problems and Developmental Disabilities

One other important aspect of self-regulation involves the ability to manage socially appropriate behavior even during frustrating or demanding situations. According to Kopp (1992), when emotional regulation and self-regulation are linked, young children learn to adopt standards for behavior and comply with caregivers' requests with positive affect. When children have persistent difficulty in regulating their emotions, they exhibit behavior problems (e.g., tantrums, defiance, or withdrawal) that often interfere with their ability to acquire new skills (Doss & Reichle, 1989), and they may become more socially isolated with increasingly fewer opportunities to engage in socially appropriate behaviors (Kaiser & Rasminsky, 1999). Children with high levels of behavior problems are particularly challenging to parents (Anderson, Lytton, & Romney, 1986), and even modest problems appear to be related to parent well-being (Warfield, Krauss, Hauser-Cram, Upshur, & Shonkoff, 1999).

Estimates of the prevalence of behavior problems in children with disabilities vary greatly. Most studies indicate a higher level in children with intellectual impairments in comparison to the general population (e.g., Jacobson, 1982). In a longitudinal study of children with mental retardation, Koller, Richardson, Katz, and McLaren (1983) reported that 61% of the children in their sample displayed some behavior problems, with 18% displaying moderate to severe disturbance. Lacharite, Boutet, and Proulx (1995) estimated that children with mental retardation are about twice as likely to develop behavioral problems in comparison to children with typical intellectual development. Children with Down syndrome, however, tend to display fewer behavior problems in areas such as mood and predictability than their typically developing peers (Gunn & Cuskelly, 1991). Therefore, high rates of behavior problems among children with developmental disabilities are not ubiquitous.

FAMILY CONTEXT AND THE DEVELOPMENT OF CHILDREN WITH DISABILITIES

Bronfenbrenner (1986) contended that although developmental processes are advanced in multiple settings (e.g., schools, religious institutions, youth organizations), the family is the "principal context in which human development takes place" (p. 723). One way in which family environments differ is in the socioeconomic resources parents provide. Strong and consistent findings exist about the relation between socioeconomic family factors and child cognitive outcomes for typically developing children (e.g., Duncan, Brooks-Gunn, & Klebanov, 1994); however, few researchers

11

have investigated this relation in children with disabilities. Moreover, little consistency has been found across the few studies in which parent education levels or similar measures of socioeconomic status (SES) have been studied for such children. Some researchers have reported a significant positive effect, with children from more highly resourced families performing significantly better (e.g., Golden & Pashayan, 1976; Sharav, Collins, & Shlomo, 1985) whereas others have not found a significant relation (e.g., Bennett, Sells, & Brand, 1979; Carr, 1995).

Although the financial and educational resources of parents logically may be expected to relate to their children's development, families with the same level of resources may exhibit quite different patterns of relationships and operational styles. Proximal family interaction patterns appear to be central to the development of children with and without developmental disabilities (Guralnick, 1997). Important dimensions within families include the emotional relationships of family members with each other and parent-child dyadic interaction (Krauss & Jacobs, 1990), processes that are hypothesized to explain variability in how families react to and adjust over time to crises and ongoing developmental stressors.

Family Emotional Climate and Children's Development

The emotional life of families is an important factor in children's development (Gottman, Katz, & Hooven, 1996). A variety of studies have been conducted examining the relation between child outcomes (such as social competence) and different aspects of the family emotional climate, such as family cohesion, the degree of independence fostered in the family, and the degree of family conflict (Wallander, Varni, Babani, Banis, & Wilcox, 1989). In this regard, family cohesiveness is considered to be a protective mechanism, especially in regard to child outcomes (National Research Council and Institute of Medicine, 2000).

Considerable research has been conducted on the relation between the familial emotional climate and the course of psychiatric disorders and maladaptive behavior in children (e.g., Pettit, Bates, & Dodge, 1993). These relations have been studied much less frequently, however, in families where a child has a developmental disability. One aspect of the family climate that has received attention is the relation of the quality of the marital relationship and the ability to form effective parenting alliances to parent-child interactions. Floyd and Zmich (1991) found that the emotional strength of the marital relationship was significantly associated with more positive parent-child exchanges.

The most extensive research on the relation between the family emotional climate and the functioning of children with mental retardation has been conducted through a series of studies by Mink, Nihira, and

12

colleagues (e.g., Mink, Blacher, & Nihira, 1988; Mink, Nihira, & Meyers, 1983; Nihira, Mink, & Meyers, 1985). Mink, Nihira, and Meyers (1983) categorized families into five distinct types based on the emotional climate, value orientation, and management style of the family. They found that families of children with mental retardation that were characterized by high levels of cohesion and harmonious interactions had children with more positive socioemotional functioning.

The importance of family cohesion in relation to children's development was also noted in analyses of the subsample of children with Down syndrome in the EICS study. We found that family processes during infancy, notably family cohesiveness and mother-child interactive behaviors, predicted growth in children's communication, social, and daily living skills over the first 5 years of life (Hauser-Cram et al., 1999).

In summary, there is an emerging literature regarding the contextual role of family relationships in the development of children with developmental disabilities, although it is not as extensive as that addressing children with psychiatric disorders or those confronting economic hardship. In contrast, one aspect of the family environment, mother-child interaction, has been studied extensively in families where a child has a developmental disability.

Mother-Child Interaction and Child Development

Although many dyadic relationships occur within families, mother-child interaction has been the one most prominently studied in the child development literature. Much of this research has been guided by a transactional framework (Sameroff & Chandler, 1975) and has emphasized that children and mothers influence each other within and across contexts and over time (Lerner, 1998).

The link between contingent and responsive growth-promoting mother-child interaction and strong child skills is well documented for young children developing typically (e.g., Bornstein & Tamis-LeMonda, 1989). Barnard (1997) described the mutual responsibilities of the child and the parent in maintaining interaction during "teaching" episodes. If the parent does the task for the child, is intrusive in the child's attempts, or ignores the child's activities, the child will not benefit. If the parent paces interactions to be responsive to a child's autonomous activity, children demonstrate cognitive advantages (Barnard & Kelly, 1990). Therefore, ideal "teaching" occurs in dyadic relationships that are mutually contingent and adaptive.

The quality of mother-child transactions is considered central to the development of all children, including those with disabilities (Guralnick, in press). Parental contingent responsiveness appears to be important in teaching-learning situations for children with disabilities just as it is for other children (McCollum & Hemmeter, 1997). However, some evidence exists that, in comparison to parents of typically developing children, parents of children with disabilities tend to be more stimulating, directive, and dominant in their interactions with the child (Marfo, 1991). Researchers have suggested that caregivers of children with disabilities tend to be more directive because children take longer to respond (Maurer & Sherrod, 1987) and display more unreadable cues (Hyche, Bakeman, & Adamson, 1992). Marfo, Dedrick, and Barbour (1998) suggested that directiveness may not necessarily be deleterious but instead may be an adaptive response to children who demonstrate less responsiveness themselves and who display less differentiated cues during interactions with others. From a transactional perspective, directiveness may be an attempt to enhance and maintain synchrony (Sameroff & Fiese, 1990). For example, Crawley and Spiker (1983) found that caregivers could be both directive and sensitive to their child's responses. Kelly and Barnard (2000) contend that the success of an interaction between a mother and a child is heavily reliant on the mother's ability to adjust her behavior in response to the child's engagement and disengagement. Rather than emphasizing maternal directives, they recommend that researchers and providers focus on the interacting system.

In summary, just as in the development of all children, family relationships, especially the mother-child dyadic relationship, play a central role in the development of young children with disabilities. As discussed in the next section, there are several theoretical vantage points that attest to the importance of viewing the family as a coherent system that affects the development of all its members—including children with disabilities—and much remains to be learned from empirical investigations of these theories.

PARENTAL ADAPTATION TO A CHILD WITH A DISABILITY

Contemporary research on the adaptation of families of children with disabilities has profited from incorporating aspects of social ecology theory, family systems theory, and family stress theory. *Social ecology theory* posits that individual development occurs within a differentiated context, including multiple environments that range from the most proximal (i.e., the individual's family) to the most distal (i.e., the larger social values of a culture) (Bronfenbrenner, 1979). Consequently, studies have examined the extent to which the quality and nature of the family environment (including the marital relationship, family cohesiveness and adaptability, and parenting styles) and the quantity and efficacy of informal and formal

14

support systems utilized by families help to explain variation in parental and family adaptation to atypical parenting experiences (Kazak, 1992). *Family systems theory* posits that within a particular social context or ecology, the family is an open, interactive system that operates according to a generalized set of principles (Minuchin, 1988). Changes in one family member affect other family members, resulting in multiple ripple effects over time. This perspective has been pivotal in expanding the focus of contemporary family research beyond a simplistic assumption of unidirectional effects of specific child characteristics on family or parental adaptation. *Family stress theory* proposes that family adaptation to a crisis event (such as having a child with a disability) is explained by multiple factors, including the nature of the crisis event, the internally (such as coping strategies) and externally (such as formal and informal support networks) based resources available, and the meaning ascribed by the family members to the event (McCubbin & Patterson, 1982). Over time, the family's adaptation to its altered circumstances changes and is affected by any one or a combination of new stressors, resources, and meanings integrated into the family that reshape its coping mechanisms.

These three major theoretical influences on family research have resulted in complex questions posed about the nature and variability in family responses to parenting a child with a disability (Ramey, Krauss, & Simeonsson, 1989). As Crnic, Friedrich, and Greenberg (1983) noted almost 20 years ago, "Family functioning cannot be considered simply as a response to a retarded child; rather, it is more meaningful to consider familial adaptation as a response to the child mediated by the coping resources available and influenced by the family's ecological environments" (p. 136). More recent perspectives have proposed a model of "resilient disruption" for families (Costigan, Floyd, Harter, & McClintock, 1997), noting that family patterns, routines, and expectations are disrupted by the birth of a child with a disability but, over time, most families regain an equilibrium in their family relationships and well-being. Seltzer and Heller (1997) note that when a child has a lifelong disability, "parenting takes on some aspects of a 'career' which may change over time as the child grows up and his or her needs and abilities change" (p. 322). Thus, contemporary scholarship underscores the value of taking a long-term perspective to the adaptation of families and the well-being of the parents. Over time, accommodations are made in family routines, expertise in managing the unique and common demands of parenting children with disabilities is developed, and coping strategies and social supports are utilized that can enhance the family's capacities to provide developmentally appropriate environments for children with disabilities.

Studies of families of children with developmental disabilities have focused on the intra- and extrafamilial context to understand why some families adjust positively, both initially and over the life course, and why other families experience greater degrees of dysfunction. With respect to intrafamilial factors, researchers have examined the relation among specific characteristics of the child (such as intensity of caregiving needs and behavior problems) (Erickson & Upshur, 1989), specific dyadic relationships (such as the parent-child, marital, and sibling relationships), the level and adequacy of financial and other resources (Floyd & Saitzyk, 1992), parental coping strategies (Frey, Greenberg, & Fewell, 1989), and the family's emotional climate as sources of variability in parental well-being (McCubbin & Huang, 1989). Studies have also targeted the relation between general negative life events and family well-being (Sameroff, Seifer, Barocas, Zax, & Greenspan, 1987). With respect to extrafamilial factors, studies have examined the role of formal and informal social support (Dunst, Trivette, & Jodry, 1997; Miller, Gordon, Daniele, & Diller, 1992). The investigation of these more complex and differentiated aspects of individual families has moved the field of family research beyond the question of whether having a child with a developmental disability affects the parents and/or the family in ways that are different from families without such atypical parenting careers. Rather, research now tries to tease out what matters for which types of families with what types of children at what periods in the family life course.

The present investigation was designed to consider the relation between children's characteristics and developmental processes and the affective environment of the family, to examine how both mothers and fathers adapt to their child with a disability, and to investigate internal (e.g., coping) and external (e.g., social support) factors that are related to differences in parent well-being over time. In order to contextualize our study within existing knowledge about parental well-being and within the heterogeneous population of families of children with developmental disabilities, we review briefly three bodies of literature: studies of parent well-being among families of children with disabilities, differences in well-being between mothers and fathers, and longitudinal studies of family adaptation.

Studies of Parent Well-Being

It is widely acknowledged that having a child with a disability presents new and often unexpected challenges, and that a variety of factors affect the course of parental adaptation (Glidden & Floyd, 1997). Well-being is conceptualized typically as having multiple components, including the parent's satisfaction with and adaptation to the child's temperamental and behavioral characteristics (commonly labeled *child-related stress*) and the parent's own emotional resources and adjustment to the parental role (commonly labeled *parent-related stress*). Investigators have examined the extent to which parents report difficulty adjusting to such child characteristics as poorer self-regulatory skills, temperamental instability, or behavioral challenges (Duis, Summers, & Summers, 1997; Innocenti, Huh, & Boyce, 1992). There is a remarkable overall consistency that parents of children with disabilities report significantly higher stress associated with the characteristics of their children than parents of typically developing children. With respect to studies of parent-related stress, investigators target the personal impacts on the parent(s) of having a child with a disability and study aspects of personal well-being such as depressive symptoms, family problems, and sense of competence as a parent (Frey et al., 1989)

Empirically, the most common approaches are either to compare the psychological well-being of parents with and without children with developmental disabilities, or to examine correlates of parent well-being. Because parent well-being is hypothesized to be affected by a variety of factors (Bradley, Rock, Whiteside, Caldwell, & Brisby, 1991), there is an increasing sophistication in the literature on identifying both direct effects and mediating or moderating factors. Specifically, studies have examined the relation between parent well-being and characteristics of the child (such as the type, severity, and functional/behavioral consequences of the disability), characteristics of the parent (such as education and financial resources), and parental resources, including the strength and supportiveness of their social networks, and the use of problem-solving coping strategies.

With respect to group differences, mothers of children with disabilities generally rate their children as having significantly more impaired temperamental characteristics related to self-regulatory processes (i.e., more distractible, more demanding, less adaptable) in comparison to mothers of children developing typically (Innocenti et al., 1992; Orr, Cameron, Dobson, & Day, 1993). These differences are persistent over time, and are most pronounced during middle childhood (ages 6–12 years) (Orr et al., 1993).

Studies that compare aspects of parent well-being between parents of children with and without disabilities have yielded mixed results. In some cases, no significant differences were found with respect to parental depression, sense of isolation, marital relationships, or sense of competence between those with and without children with disabilities (Gowen, Johnson-Martin, Goldman, & Appelbaum, 1989; Harris & McHale, 1989; Innocenti et al., 1992; Orr et al., 1993). Others (notably older studies) have reported significant differences between those with and without children with disabilities in parental depressive symptoms, levels of malaise, and dysphoric affect (Breslau & Davis, 1986).

A large body of research generally concludes that parent well-being is lower among parents (typically mothers) of children with more extensive caretaking needs, more severe disabilities, and more difficult temperaments and/or behavior problems (McKinney & Peterson, 1987). It has also been reported that parental distress is greater for parents of boys with disabilities and for children with poorer communication skills (Frey et al., 1989). Parent well-being is consistently better among parents with strong and satisfying social support networks (Dunst et al., 1997) and among those with problem-focused coping styles (i.e., active, planful approaches to stress) in comparison to those with emotion-focused coping styles (i.e., venting of feelings, behavioral withdrawal) (Bradley et al., 1991; Judge, 1998).

Duis et al. (1997) integrated family systems theory and social ecological theory in their study of parents of preschool-aged children and found that parent well-being among two-parent families of children without disabilities and families of children with Down syndrome were similar and were higher in comparison to families of children with hearing impairments or developmental delay as well as single-parent families of children without disabilities. They also found that overall parent well-being was more strongly associated with child characteristics among parents of children with disabilities in comparison to parents of children without disabilities (regardless of marital status). For parents of children without disabilities, parent well-being was most highly associated with family cohesion, a relation that was not found among families of children with disabilities.

Comparisons of Maternal and Paternal Well-Being

Mothers are usually the primary caregivers of their children, including children with disabilities, and have been the primary focus of studies on parent well-being, but there is increasing interest in exploring differences in maternal and paternal well-being among parents of children with disabilities. The literature on fathers of children with disabilities, however, is much less extensive than that on mothers (Lamb & Billings, 1997). Early investigations focused on fathers' supportiveness toward their wives as a factor in maternal well-being (Bristol, Gallagher, & Schopler, 1988), an issue of particular importance in light of findings that fathers tend to maintain traditional, gender-based division of labor within families of children with disabilities (Erickson & Upshur, 1989; Lamb & Billings, 1997).

Several studies have found that mothers and fathers of children with disabilities generally report similar levels of personal well-being, although the factors that influence paternal and maternal well-being are different (Dyson, 1997; Krauss, 1993; Roach, Orsmond, & Barratt, 1999). Krauss (1993) found that fathers' well-being was sensitive to their child's temperament, their relationship with the child, and the quality of the family environment. In contrast, mothers' well-being was associated with the personal challenges of being a parent and the helpfulness of their social support networks. Dyson (1997) found that although fathers and mothers of children with disabilities did not differ in levels of parental stress, social support, or family functioning, parental stress was related to family problems due to the child's special needs, to the family's emotional climate, and to parents' pessimism concerning the child's future. Roach et al. (1999) found that mothers and fathers of children with Down syndrome gave similar ratings with respect to their child's caregiving difficulties, child-related stress, parent-related stress, and involvement in the child's daily care. They also noted that very few parents had levels of parental stress that were clinically significant, suggesting that parental adaptation rather than parental dysfunction is common among parents of children with Down syndrome.

Longitudinal Studies of Parental Adaptation

There is little controversy that the diagnosis of child disability initially provokes intense, jarring, and often debilitating reactions among parents. The psychological assault that most parents experience in learning that their infant or toddler has a significant developmental anomaly is powerfully evident in the literature written by parents (e.g., Featherstone, 1980). A lens that is restricted to the early diagnostic period, however, misses the fact that parenting a child with a disability is a changing, lifelong process (Seltzer & Heller, 1997). Researchers have become increasingly interested in understanding the life course experiences of parents of children with disabilities, and longitudinal studies now provide instructive findings about variability in family experiences (Seltzer, Greenberg, Floyd, Pette, & Hong, 2001).

Gowen et al. (1989) examined maternal depression and feelings of parenting competence longitudinally among mothers of handicapped and nonhandicapped infants assessed multiple times during infancy. Despite notable differences in the caregiving needs of the two groups of infants, there were no significant differences in feelings of depression or parenting competence between their mothers. Further, among both groups of mothers, about half evidenced clinically significant depressive symptoms at least once in the series of assessment points. These findings suggest a waxing and waning pattern of maternal depression in response to the challenge of having an infant (with or without disabilities). In contrast, feelings of parenting competence and quality of family relationships were stable over time in both groups.

Hanson and Hanline (1990) followed a small sample of mothers of children with disabilities for 3 years. They reported no significant changes in maternal ratings for child-related or parent-related stress. This suggests remarkable stability of maternal adjustment. However, they also found that mothers of less developmentally advanced children reported more stress.

Dyson (1993) investigated stability and change in parental stress and family functioning over 4 years, and attempted to identify factors contributing to differences in homes with and without children with disabilities. Families were matched initially for age of the child (all were under 6 years of age), family socioeconomic status, and marital status. She found no significant change over 4 years in overall parent well-being and family functioning for either group of families. However, parents of children with disabilities had significantly higher parental stress than families of children without disabilities. She also reported that parental stress at follow-up for the former group was associated with the quality of family relationships and degree of family cohesion, whereas family functioning was not related to changes in parental well-being for the latter group.

We investigated mothers in the EICS when their children with disabilities were at ages less than 1 year (on average), 3 years, and 5 years (Warfield et al., 1999). We found rather dramatic increases over time in the percentage of mothers who warranted clinical referral because of high levels of stress associated with their children's functioning and temperamental characteristics (such as demandingness, stability of mood, and adaptability). We also found, however, that aspects of the family ecology, such as more economic and social resources and greater family emotional cohesiveness, were highly and positively associated with greater levels of parent well-being.

Gallimore and colleagues conducted a longitudinal study of the functional accommodations in daily routines made by families of children with nonspecific developmental delays (Gallimore, Coots, Weisner, Garnier, & Guthrie, 1996; Gallimore, Keogh, & Bernheimer, 1999). They found that although families report substantially more types of accommodations as their children grow older, the intensity of their accommodations remains stable between ages 3 to 7 and decreases significantly from ages 7 to 11. They also found lower child competencies associated with more intense family accommodation activities, but noted that the level of family accommodations was not associated with changes in the child's competencies (Keogh, Garnier, Bernheimer, & Gallimore, 2000).

Thus, the limited number of longitudinal studies suggest that both mothers and fathers make positive adaptations to their child's special needs and do not evidence clinically significant levels of depression or parental stress, at least in the early childhood period. In addition, parent well-being appears to be related to the psychosocial and connected aspects of the family. Studies also demonstrate, however, that as children with disabilities age, their parents report increasing amounts of difficulty with their child's developmental process, especially in regard to temperament and self-regulatory behaviors.

CONCEPTUAL APPROACH

Considered as a whole, studies of children with disabilities and their families indicate that family processes and children's development are mutually interrelated. Research on very young children points to the central role of mother-child interaction and, although less studied, the importance of the emotional climate of the family in promoting optimal child development. Children's characteristics (e.g., age, functional skills, behavioral regulation) also are associated with how parents' accommodate to the process of caring for a child with disabilities. Thus, children and parents constitute an integrated, relational system, in which subsystems interact, and each subsystem, through its fusion with the whole, also influences its own well-being (Overton, 1998; Thalen & Smith, 1998). Children with more highly developed self-regulating processes advance their own learning and development, and families with strong intrafamilial relationships and extrafamilial supports promote the emotional well-being of their members. Thus, the process of change for both children with disabilities and their parents is dynamic and involves elements of agency and interrelatedness (Brandstädter, 1998; Magnusson & Stattin, 1998).

Longitudinal investigations, however, are lacking and no single investigation has incorporated the multiple sets of relations purported to be important to both optimal child development and parent adaptation. Moreover, the patterns reported here suggest that a developmental-contextual systems perspective would offer an important new comprehensive understanding of the development of children with developmental disabilities and the adaptation of their parents. Developmental-contextual systems theory is based on the following tenets: (a) the basic processes of development are relational; (b) development is relatively plastic and a result of the fusion of nature and nurture rather than the product of either; (c) humans are active agents of their own development; and (d) development occurs within multiple hierarchical contexts that are reciprocally related (Ford & Lerner, 1992; Lerner, 1998; Overton, 1998; Thalen & Smith, 1998). The study reported here tests conceptual models constructed from this perspective, and advances our understanding of development in children with disabilities and adaptation among their parents from a view in which relations are considered reciprocal and changing.

III. THE EARLY INTERVENTION COLLABORATIVE STUDY: STUDY DESIGN AND METHODOLOGY

In this chapter we discuss the conceptual models that have guided this research and were developed from theoretical and empirical work in child development, family systems, and developmental disabilities. We then describe the EICS sample, study design, and procedures for data collection. Next, we report the variables and measures selected to operationalize the constructs in the conceptual models. Finally, we describe the analysis strategy and method for presenting the findings.

CONCEPTUAL MODELS

This research was guided by two related conceptual models (Figures 1 and 2) that were constructed based on a developmental-contextual perspective. The models include child and family characteristics and processes measured when the child was age 3, which serve both as correlates of child and parent behavioral status at age 3, and as predictors of trajectories of children's development and parent well-being over the entire study period (from infancy/toddlerhood to age 10 years). Age 3 measurements were selected as predictors because this is the time when program transitions occur. Children and parents enter early intervention programs during the child's infant or toddler years, and they leave at 3 years of age. Those who remain in need of special services enter special education supported by the public schools. Therefore, it is critical to determine the characteristics and processes that at 3 years of age predict children's development and parent well-being. From the perspective of service provision, if children with particular developmental skills or processes fare better over time, it would seem prudent for future early intervention and school-based services to focus on helping children develop those skills or processes. Further, if parents of children with particular needs demonstrate poorer well-being over time, then early intervention and school-based services should focus intensively on addressing those needs.

From a developmental-contextual systems perspective, the analyses derived from the models were designed to test the extent to which children promote their own development, the extent to which the parental system may account for changes in the child's development beyond that given by child agency, and the extent to which children's specific characteristics and family processes may account for changes in parent well-being over time. Thus, we were interested in examining the bidirectional relations of parent to child and child to parent.

Mental age and adaptive behavior were selected as child outcome measures (Figure 1). These domains were selected because of their importance to the child's school and life skills. Three domains of adaptive behavior were examined: social skills, communication skills, and daily living skills. As described in more detail in the analysis section, we developed and tested models to examine the correlates of the child's functioning at the end of the early intervention period (at child age 3) and to predict change in these skills during the early to middle childhood period.

Predictors of child outcome measures include the type of disability (Down syndrome, motor impairment, or developmental delay), other child characteristics (gender and health), and parent characteristics (education level, marital status). It was hypothesized that after accounting for child and parent characteristics, child outcomes would be related to both child and family *processes*. Specifically, based on the literature on children's self-regulatory processes (reviewed in chapter II), we hypothesized that mastery motivation and behavior regulation would be correlated with mental age and adaptive behavior at age 3 and would predict changes in these domains over time. It was further hypothesized that, beyond self-regulatory processes, family climate would be a significant correlate of the child's developmental functioning at age 3 and would be a predictor of developmental progress over time. The family forms the proximal setting in which the young child develops, and the literature (reviewed in chapter II) led us to delineate two key aspects of the family climate: mother-child interaction and the social-emotional tenor of family relations. We posited that children demonstrate more positive developmental trajectories if they live in families in which mothers are growth-promoting in their interactive skills and family social-emotional relationships are mutually supportive (Figure 1).

Parent well-being (Figure 2) includes child-related and parent-related stress, each measured separately for mothers and fathers. Child-related stress includes aspects of the child's temperament related to self-regulatory behaviors, such as demandingness, adaptability, and mood, that a parent finds troublesome. Parent-related stress includes aspects of the parenting experience that result in instability in a parent's emotional equilibrium, such as social isolation, depression, strained relationship with spouse, and

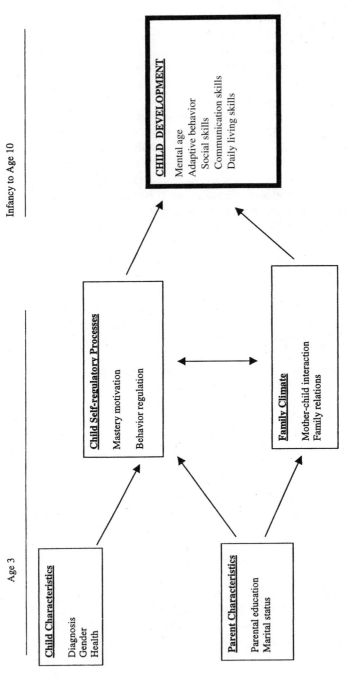

Age 3

Infancy to Age 10

CHILD DEVELOPMENT

Mental age
Adaptive behavior
Social skills
Communication skills
Daily living skills

Child Self-regulatory Processes

Mastery motivation

Behavior regulation

Child Characteristics

Diagnosis
Gender
Health

Family Climate

Mother-child interaction
Family relations

Parent Characteristics

Parental education
Marital status

FIGURE 1.—Conceptual model for predictors of children's development. Arrows indicate expected relations.

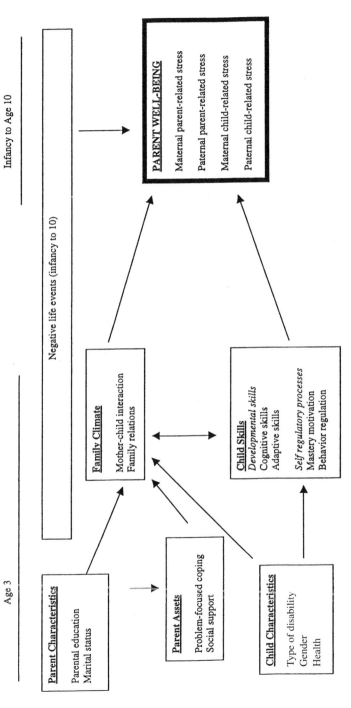

FIGURE 2.—Conceptual model for predictors of parent well-being. Arrows indicate expected relations.

poor health. Because other situations, such as the accumulation of debt or marital breakup, can also relate to well-being, we controlled for those negative life events that occurred over the entire study period. Therefore, the focus of the analyses was on family, child, and parenting experiences that relate to parent well-being.

As the model indicates, we expected specific parent characteristics (i.e., education and marital status) and child characteristics (i.e., type of disability, gender, and health) to relate to parent well-being. Beyond family and child characteristics, we predicted that parent assets, specifically problem-focused coping strategies and social support, would correlate with parent well-being and predict changes in well-being over time. We further hypothesized that the family climate, specifically mother-child interaction and family social-emotional relationships, would correlate with parent well-being and would predict change in the well-being of mothers and fathers. Finally, we hypothesized that children's developmental skills and self-regulatory behaviors would significantly predict the well-being of both mothers and fathers. Thus, as indicated in the model (Figure 2), we hypothesized that parent assets, the family climate, and children's skills and processes all have a significant relation to parental well-being. Models combining mother and father data were estimated (as opposed to analyzing separate models for each parent) to account for the high correlation between partners' trajectories of stress.

THE SAMPLE

Study participants were recruited from 29 community-based early intervention programs in Massachusetts and New Hampshire. Parents were asked to participate if their child had Down syndrome (and was no older than 12 months of age), motor impairment (and was no older than 24 months of age), or developmental delay of unknown etiology (and was no older than 24 months of age). The diagnosis of children with Down syndrome was confirmed by a review of the medical records. Children with motor impairment were selected to participate if they had evidence of abnormal muscle tone (hypotonia, hypertonia, or fluctuating tone) or a coordination deficit along with delayed or deviant motor development, with or without other delays. Children with developmental delay were selected to participate if they had evidence of delays in two or more areas of development, with no established diagnosis or etiology that implied a specific diagnosis at the time of entry into early intervention services.

A total of 190 children were recruited for the first phase of this study (i.e., the first year of participation in an early intervention program), the results of which were reported in a previous *SRCD Monograph* (Shonkoff et al., 1992). The longitudinal investigation reported here was based on a sample of 183 children and their parents. For these analyses, the sample of children with motor impairment was restricted to children who had motor impairment at both study entry and at age 3 years. The sample of children with developmental delay was restricted to children who evidenced delay in two areas of development at study entry and at age 3. Thus, children identified originally as motor impaired or developmentally delayed at study entry but who no longer fit into any of the three disability groups by age 3 were eliminated from the analyses.

Demographic information on the longitudinal sample of children and families at the time of exit from early intervention (age 3 years) is reported in Table 1. The sample had a larger proportion of children with motor impairment than children in the other two groups and a slightly higher proportion of males than females. The predominant ethnic group was European American, and, on average, mothers and fathers had almost 14 years of education. The majority of parents were married, and the majority of children lived with both parents. Some of the demographic characteristics differed by disability group. Mothers of children with Down syndrome were more likely to be employed, fathers of children with motor impairment were less likely to be married although almost three quarters were married (74.6%), fathers of children with Down syndrome had completed more years of education than fathers of children with developmental delay, and children with Down syndrome tended to be in families with a larger number of children.

The sample was constructed originally to represent the three most common categories of disability served by early intervention programs in Massachusetts. However, since the beginning of the study in 1985, the population of early intervention programs across the nation has changed. In comparing the EICS sample to a current representative national sample of children and families in early intervention (Hebbeler et al., 2001), several differences are apparent. Specifically, although the gender distribution is similar, the EICS sample has a higher proportion of European-American children and a lower proportion of Hispanics, African Americans, and other ethnic groups. Second, children considered "at risk" for poor developmental outcomes but without evidence of delay were not included in the EICS sample, although they represent 17% of the national sample. Third, rates of public assistance are lower in the EICS sample compared to rates in the national sample.

In comparison to the U.S. population of comparable age at a comparable time, the EICS sample participants were more highly educated (13.7% of mothers and 14.6% of fathers had a graduate degree in comparison to 5.7% of females and 9.0% of males in the U.S. population; 8.2% of mothers and 13.5% of fathers in the EICS sample did not have a high school

27

TABLE 1

DEMOGRAPHIC CHARACTERISTICS OF EICS PARTICIPANTS
AT AGE 3 YEARS ($N = 183$)

Characteristics	%	M	(SD)
Child			
Type of disability			
Down syndrome	32.8		
Motor impairment	39.3		
Developmental delay	27.9		
Gender			
Male	57.4		
Racial/ethnic origin			
European American	89.1		
African American	1.6		
Hispanic	4.9		
Mixed race/other	4.4		
Lives with both parents	82.3		
First born	39.4		
Family			
Income (1989–91)			
Less than 10K	14.3		
Between 10 and 20K	11.8		
Between 20 and 30K	22.4		
More than 30K	51.6		
Number of children		2.2	(1.0)
Mother			
Education (years)		13.8	(2.5)
Marital status (married)	80.7		
Employment (employed)	48.5		
Father			
Education (years)		13.7	(3.1)
Marital status (married)	83.7		
Employment (employed)	90.2		

diploma compared to 24.2% of women and 24.3% of men nationally; U.S. Bureau of the Census, 1990). Also, fewer children in the EICS sample lived in poverty in comparison to other children in the United States. For example, 16.3% of children in the EICS sample were eligible for a free school lunch. This percentage is higher than the figure for New Hampshire where 12.4% of children were eligible, but lower than that of other adjacent states, such as Rhode Island (28%) or Connecticut (20.3%) (U.S. Department of Education, 1996–97). Unfortunately, comparable data were not available for Massachusetts. A slightly higher rate of married-couple–headed households was evident in the EICS sample (80.7% of mothers) in comparison to that reported for U.S. households (78.4%) (U.S. Bureau of the Census, 1992). Additionally, a higher proportion of study participants reported their descent as European American (89.1% of EICS participants) in comparison to that of the U.S. population (80.0%) (U.S. Bureau of the Census, 1990).

At age 3 years, a large proportion of children in the sample (89.7%) entered public school-supported services for children with special needs. At age 10, all but 10 children in the sample had Individualized Education Plans (IEPs). Thus, almost all children in this sample had early special needs and continued to exhibit special needs during the early and middle childhood periods. To illustrate this point, Table 2 lists aspects of adaptive behavior for the EICS sample in terms of children's success with typical tasks at ages 3, 5, and 10 years.

As noted in the table, although many of the children in the sample had motor problems, almost all were able to walk on their own. In contrast, fewer were able to accomplish the more complex motor task of bicycle riding. Only some children were able to succeed by age 10 at typical school-related tasks such as telling time and reading. Perhaps most striking is the finding that only one third of the children in the sample were reported to have a group of friends at age 10.

TABLE 2

SELECTED ADAPTIVE SKILLS OF CHILDREN AT AGES 3, 5, AND 10 YEARS

	Percentage "usually or always"[a]		
	Age 3	Age 5	Age 10
Daily living skills			
Feeds self with spoon	73.3	88.6	91.3
Urinates in toilet	19.4	60.4	82.6
Dresses self	1.2	13.4	60.1
States day of week	0	1.3	44.9
Tells time	0	0	23.9
Socialization skills			
Has a group of friends	0	4.7	31.2
Plays board games	0	12.1	50.7
Communication skills			
Uses nouns and verbs	47.9	77.9	81.9
Prints own name	0	4.7	62.3
Reads (second-grade level)	0	0	39.1
Motor skills			
Walks	80.6	86.6	89.8
Cuts with scissors	6.7	46.3	78.3
Rides bicycle	0	.7	29.7

[a]Based on maternal report using the Vineland Scales (Sparrow et al., 1984).

29

STUDY DESIGN

This study was designed as a prospective, longitudinal, nonexperimental investigation of children with developmental disabilities and their parents. A primary goal was to generate and test conceptual models of child and family development that include hypothesized predictors of change in children's capacities and parent well-being.

Data were collected at five times, from the child's entry into early intervention services during the infant or toddler years and continuing through age 10. The first time of measurement, T1, occurred within 6 weeks of entry to early intervention; the second was 1 year later (T2). Because children with disabilities enter early intervention at different ages, children's ages at T1 and T2 varied by type of disability. At T1, children with Down syndrome were a mean age of 3.8 months ($SD = 3.2$), children with motor impairment were a mean age of 11.8 months ($SD = 4.4$), and children with developmental delay were a mean age of 16.1 months ($SD = 5.6$) ($F = 110.9$, $p < .001$). On average, children in each of the three groups were 12 months older at T2 (Down syndrome $M = 15.9$, $SD = 3.2$; motor impairment $M = 23.9$, $SD = 4.5$; developmental delay $M = 27.9$, $SD = 5.5$). Beginning at the third time of measurement (T3), children's ages did not vary significantly by type of disability. The third measurement (T3) occurred when children were age 3 years (36 months); the fourth (T4) occurred when children were age 5 years (60 months), and the fifth (T5) occurred when they were age 10 years (120 months).

PROCEDURE

The measurement procedures for each of the times of measurement were quite similar. Two field staff members trained to be reliable for all measures used in data collection and blind to the study hypotheses conducted a home visit. One staff member conducted a multidimensional, structured evaluation of the child, which included a standard developmental assessment (e.g., the Bayley Scales of Infant Development) at all times of measurement, an observational assessment of mastery motivation (at T3), and an observational assessment of mother-child interaction (at T3). The second staff member conducted an interview with the mother. At each time of measurement, this interview included an evaluation of the child's adaptive behavior, questions about demographic information, questionnaire data, and specific questions about raising a child who had early special needs. The second staff member also observed and recorded (for reliability) the mother-child interaction task. If either the mother or child was experiencing an atypical day, the home visit was rescheduled for another time. The mother was sent a packet of questionnaires before the home visit, which a staff member collected during the home visit. An identical packet of self-administered questionnaires was also brought to the home visit and left for the child's father to complete independently. On average, home visits took approximately 2 to 3 hours to complete.

VARIABLES

A variety of measures were used to operationalize the constructs included in the conceptual models. Table 3 lists the study variables and measures as well as information on data collection methods. Table 4 presents descriptive information (i.e., mean, standard deviation, and range) on the predictor variables at age 3.

Outcome Measures: Children's Development (Infancy to Age 10 Years)

Mental age. Several different age-appropriate instruments were used to assess the child's mental age over the five data points. At T1 and T2 (i.e., the first year in early intervention), the Mental Scale of the Bayley Scales of Infant Development (Bayley, 1969) was used for all children. At T3 and T4 (ages 3 and 5 years) the McCarthy Scales of Children's Abilities (McCarthy, 1972) and at T5 (age 10 years) the Stanford-Binet Intelligence Scale (Thorndike, Hagen, & Sattler, 1986) were used where appropriate. A small subgroup of children (approximately 15%) was assessed using the Bayley Scales at each time point. Mental age equivalent scores on these measures were calculated based on tables in the manuals of each measure and used in the analyses. Reliabilities ranged from .80 to .97.

Adaptive skills. The Vineland Adaptive Behavior Scales-Interview Form (Sparrow, Balla, & Cicchetti, 1984) were used to assess child functioning in three domains: social, communication, and daily living. Motor skills were also assessed using the Vineland scales; however, because development in this domain is only measured up to 6 years of age, the scores were not analyzed in this study. The Vineland is a 577-item questionnaire measuring individual personal and social competence from birth through adulthood. In this study, a semi-structured interview was conducted during each home visit with each child's mother to identify skills the child demonstrated on a regular basis (e.g., the use of complete sentences in communicating, the development of friendships, skills related to dressing, eating, and toileting). Age equivalent scores were developed based on instructions in the manual developed for this measure. Cronbach's alpha

31

TABLE 3

Study Variables and Measures

Variables	Measures	Data Collection Method
Dependent variables		
Child mental age	Bayley Scales of Infant Development (Bayley, 1969)	Child assessment
	McCarthy Scales of Children's Abilities (McCarthy, 1972)	
	Stanford-Binet Intelligence Scale (Thorndike et al., 1986)	
Child adaptive skills	Vineland Adaptive Behavior Scales–Interview Form (Sparrow et al., 1984)	Mother interview
Child-related stress	Parenting Stress Index (Abidin, 1995)	Questionnaire (M/F)
Parent-related stress	Parenting Stress Index (Abidin, 1995)	Questionnaire (M/F)
Age 3 child characteristics		
Type of disability	Medical record review	Classification criteria
	Vineland Adaptive Behavior Scales–Interview Form (Sparrow et al., 1984)	Mother interview
Gender	EICS Information Form	Mother interview
Health	Medical record review	Number of doctor visits during the first 3 years
Age 3 parent characteristics		
Parent education	EICS Demographic Form	Questionnaire (M/F)
Marital status	EICS Demographic Form	Questionnaire (M/F)
Age 3 child self-regulatory processes		
Behavior regulation	Child Behavior Checklist for Ages 2–3 (Achenbach & Edelbrock, 1983)	Mother interview
	Classroom Problem Checklist (Kohn, 1988)	Teacher questionnaire
Mastery motivation	Individualized Assessment of Mastery Motivation (Morgan et al., 1992)	Child assessment
Age 3 child developmental skills		
Cognitive skills	McCarthy Scales of Children's Abilities (McCarthy, 1972)	Child assessment
Adaptive skills	Vineland Adaptive Behavior Scales–Interview Form (Sparrow et al., 1984)	Mother interview
Age 3 family climate		
Mother-child interaction	Nursing Child Assessment Teaching Scale (NCATS) (Barnard, 1978)	Child assessment
Family relations	Family Environment Scale (FES) (Moos, 1974)	Questionnaire (M/F)
Age 3 parent assets		
Problem-focused coping	Ways of Coping Checklist (Folkman & Lazarus, 1980)	Questionnaire (M/F)
Social support	EICS Parent Support Scale (Adapted from Dunst et al., 1984)	Questionnaire (M/F)

TABLE 4

PARTICIPANT DATA ON PREDICTOR VARIABLES AT AGE 3 YEARS

Constructs and Variables[a]	M	SD	Range
Child self-regulatory processes			
Mastery motivation			
Puzzles	38.82	30.76	0–100
Cause-effect	58.97	34.80	0–100
Behavior problems			
CBC Total Problems T Score (M)	50.47	9.53	28–79
Kohn Apathy-Withdrawal Score (T)	54.36	9.01	41–91
Kohn Anger-Defiance Score (T)	49.54	8.54	41–85
Family climate			
NCATS	37.74	6.12	15–49
Family Relations Index (M)	11.28	3.62	0–18
Family Relations Index (F)	10.54	3.82	0–17
Parent assets			
Problem-focused coping (M)	.57	.09	.32–.84
Problem-focused coping (F)	.57	.10	.21–.83
Support helpfulness (M)	27.75	9.37	11–52
Support helpfulness (F)	27.16	9.64	0–52
Child development skills			
Cognitive skills (standard score)	60.00	22.90	21–124
Adaptive behavior (standard score)	63.78	11.57	40–100

[a](M) indicates mother score, (T) indicates teacher report, and (F) indicates father score.

reliability coefficients were calculated for each of the three domains at each time point. The coefficients from T1 through T5 for communication skills were .89, .94, .95, .96, and .98. The coefficients from T1 through T5 for daily living skills were .87, .89, .91, .95, and .98. The coefficients from T1 through T5 for social skills were .89, .86, .89, .93, and .97.

Outcome Measures: Parent Well-Being (Infancy to Age 10 Years)

Maternal and paternal child-related stress. Child-related stress is conceptualized as characteristics of the child's temperament related to self-regulation and social acceptability that the parent finds difficult. The Child Domain of the PSI was used to measure child-related stress. The child domain is a 47-item scale that measures the respondent's perceived difficulty with the child's moodiness, demandingness, and adaptability (e.g., "My child is so active that it exhausts me"), reinforcement of the parent (e.g., "Sometimes I feel my child doesn't like me and doesn't want to be close to me"), and acceptability (e.g., "My child does a few things which bother me a great deal"). Child-related stress scores are calculated by summing across six subscale scores (adaptability, acceptability, demand-ingness, mood, distractibility, and reinforces parent). The Cronbach's alpha reliability coefficients for child-related stress for mothers between T1 and T5 were .89, .87, .90, .92, and .92. The Cronbach's alpha reliability coefficients for child-related stress for fathers between T1 and T5 were .86, .89, .90, .92, and .92.

The Child Domain score and individual subscales have been shown to significantly correlate with other measures of stress within the parent-child system, including the Home Situations Questionnaire ($r = .68$) (Breen & Barkley, 1988) and parent perceptions of child difficulties, such as the ADHD Rating Scale ($r = .64$ with the distractibility subscale) (Anastopoulos et al. 1992).

Maternal and paternal parent-related stress. The Parent Domain of the PSI (Abidin, 1995) was used to measure parent-related stress. The parent domain is a 54-item self-administered Likert scale that includes statements regarding the respondent's reactions to the experience of being a parent (e.g., "I feel trapped by my responsibilities as a parent") and sense of emotional equilibrium associated with the parent experience (e.g., "I often feel guilty about the way I feel toward my child"). Parent-related stress scores are calculated by summing across seven subscale scores (depression, attachment, restrictions in role, sense of competence, social isolation, relations with spouse, and parent health). The Cronbach's alpha reliability coefficients for parent-related stress for mothers between T1 and T5 were .92, .93, .93, .92, and .92. The Cronbach's alpha reliability coefficients for parent-reltated stress for fathers were .92, .93, .93, .94, and .92.

The Parent Domain has been correlated with several well-known measures of psychological distress, including the State Trait Anxiety Scale ($r = .78$ State Scale and $r = .82$ Trait Scale) (Abidin, 1983), and the Beck Depression Inventory ($r = .57$) (Breen & Barkley, 1988). Several subscales also have been shown to correlate significantly with the Center for Epidemiological Studies-Depression Scale (CES-D) (Quittner, Glueckauf, & Jackson, 1990) and the Symptom Checklist 90-Revised (Anastopoulos, Guevremont, Shelton, & DuPaul, 1992).

Age 3 Predictors of Child's Later Development

Child characteristics. Both type of disability and gender were used as predictors. As described earlier, children were categorized into one of three disability groups: (1) Down syndrome, (2) motor impairment, and (3) developmental delay. The following definitions were used to determine type of disability. Children with Down syndrome had their diagnosis confirmed through medical record review. Children with motor impairment demonstrated evidence of abnormal muscle tone (hypotonia or hypertonia) or coordination deficit, along with delayed or deviant motor development, with or without other areas of delay upon their entry to an early intervention program and had a motor age equivalent score of less than 30 months on the Vineland at age 3 years. Children with developmental delay demonstrated evidence of delays in two or more areas of development with no established diagnosis or cause that implied a specific prognosis upon their entry into an early intervention program, and had age equivalent scores of less than 30 months on two or more subscales of the Vineland (i.e., communication, daily living, social, and motor) at age 3 years. Health was assessed as the number of doctor visits made during the first 3 years of life. These data were gathered through medical record review.

Parent characteristics. Parent education attainment and marital status (i.e., married or not married) were used as potential predictors. The average of the mothers' and fathers' years of education was used as the index of parent education. Although different strategies have been suggested for combining mother and father data, average scores are considered appropriate when the scores are highly correlated (Larsen & Olson, 1990). In the EICS sample, mother and father years of education were strongly correlated ($r = .67$, $p < .001$).

Child self-regulatory processes. Self-regulatory skills include behavior regulation and mastery motivation. Behavior regulation was based on behavior problems; children with more behavior problems were considered to have lower levels of behavior regulation. Two variables were used to measure behavior regulation in order to incorporate data about behavior problems from different observers (i.e., mothers and teachers) based in different settings (i.e., the home and the classroom). When her child was 3 years of age, each mother completed the Child Behavior Checklist for Ages 2–3 (CBCL/2-3) (Achenbach & Edelbrock, 1983), and the total behavior problems score constituted one of the two behavior regulation variables investigated in the model. The Cronbach's alpha reliability coefficient for the mother-reported behavior problems score was .91. Around the same time, the child's preschool teacher completed the Classroom Problem Checklist (Kohn, 1988). The two domain scores, apathy-withdrawal (Cronbach's alpha reliability coefficient = .97) and anger-defiance (Cronbach's alpha reliability coefficient = .98), were moderately but significantly correlated ($r = .22$, $p < .05$). They were summed to create the second behavior regulation variable (i.e., the teacher-reported behavior regulation score). The total behavior regulation scores from the CBCL and the Kohn were also significantly correlated ($r = .19$, $p < .05$), but were analyzed as separate variables.

A composite measure of mastery motivation was also created. The observational measure developed by Morgan, Busch-Rossnagel, Maslin-Cole, and Harmon (1992) was used. Children were presented with two kinds of problem-posing toys: one set involved cause-effect (e.g., slide a lever to make a figure emerge) and another set involved puzzles. Both sets of toys were commercially produced and formed a hierarchy of task difficulty. The cause-effect toys included (in order of increasing difficulty): (1) a simple typewriter, (2) a surprise box, (3) a cash register, and (4) a tape recorder. The puzzles formed five levels of difficulty: (1) a balloon puzzle with six identical pieces, (2) a traffic light puzzle with six simple-shaped pieces, (3) a traffic signs puzzle with five complex geometric pieces, (4) a transportation puzzle with eight complex pieces, and (5) a three pigs puzzle with 11 interlocking pieces. Children were presented one toy from each set that was considered to be moderately challenging. Moderate challenge was defined as the child's completing at least one, but not all, solutions during the first $1\frac{1}{2}$ minutes. If the child completed all solutions within that period of time, a more challenging toy was presented; if the child was unable to complete a solution within $1\frac{1}{2}$ minutes, a less challenging toy was presented. Children's persistence on each task was scored every 15 seconds for a total of 4 minutes, yielding two scores: persistence (i.e., percentage of intervals with task persistence) on the cause-effect and on the puzzle-type tasks. There was a moderate correlation between these two scores ($r = .41$, $p < .001$). The scores from each task were converted into Z scores and summed to create the mastery motivation score.

Family climate. Two constructs were included as key aspects of the family climate. First, mother-child interaction was assessed using the Nursing Child Assessment Teaching Scale (NCATS) (Barnard, 1978). This observational rating scale was designed to assess a teaching interaction between a mother and her child. A task just beyond the child's ability level was selected for the mother to teach the child. The score, representing the mother's interaction with her child, consists of 50 items and is based on four subscales: sensitivity to cues, response to distress, social-emotional growth fostering, and cognitive growth fostering. The Cronbach's alpha reliability coefficient was .82.

The second family climate measure was the family relations index from the Family Environment Scale (FES) (Moos, 1974). This index is calculated by summing the scores for the cohesion and expressiveness subscales and subtracting the score for the conflict subscale. Both mothers and fathers completed the form independently. The Cronbach's alpha reliability coefficient for the index was .69 for mothers and .70 for fathers. The mothers' and fathers' scores on the family relations index were moderately correlated ($r = .32$, $p < .01$); an average of the two index scores was created.

Predictors at Age 3 Years of Parent Well-Being

Child characteristics. The same three characteristics (type of disability, gender, and health) that were used in the analysis of child outcomes were assessed as predictors of parent well-being.

Parent characteristics. The same two characteristics (maternal and paternal education and marital status) that were used in the analysis of child outcomes were assessed as predictors of parent well-being.

Parent assets. Two parent assets were measured. First, problem-focused coping was measured using the Ways of Coping Checklist, which was completed independently by both mothers and fathers when their child was 3 years old (Folkman & Lazarus, 1980). This scale measures the extent to which people engage in problem-focused or emotion-focused coping when faced with a stressful situation. The problem-focused coping domain includes strategies such as making a plan of action, analyzing the problem, and redoubling effort. The emotion-focused coping domain includes strategies such as denial, behavioral or emotional withdrawal, or venting emotions. The Cronbach's alpha reliability coefficients for the problem-focused domain were .83 and .86 for mothers and fathers, respectively. For the emotion-focused domain, the Cronbach's alpha reliability coefficients were .87 and .91 for mothers and fathers, respectively. Because people often use more than one coping strategy, raw scores that simply sum the items in each domain are biased by the total number of efforts endorsed across domains and thus do not reflect an emphasis on specific strategies (Vitaliano, Maiuro, Russo, & Becker, 1987). Therefore, in the analysis, a problem-focused relative score was used which measures the percentage of total effort made on problem-focused strategies.

The second asset, social support helpfulness, was utilized using a scale adapted from the 18-item Family Support Scale developed by Dunst, Jenkins, and Trivette (1984). This scale lists a variety of sources of formal and informal support and includes a 5-point Likert scale to measure the degree of helpfulness that the respondent attributes to each source. Both mothers and fathers completed this scale independently when their child was 3 years old. The Cronbach's alpha reliability coefficient was .89 and .93 for mothers and fathers, respectively.

Family climate. The same two constructs (mother-child interaction and family relations) that were employed in the analysis of child outcomes were also used in the analysis of parent well-being.

Child skills. Two types of skills were analyzed. First, the child's cognitive skills were assessed at age 3 years using either the McCarthy Scales of Children's Abilities (McCarthy, 1972) or the Bayley Scales of Infant Development (Bayley, 1969) to generate standard scores. The child's adaptive skills were measured as the total adaptive behavior score on the Vineland scales, which is a composite of the scores from the instrument's four domains: communication, daily living, motor, and social skills. The Cronbach's alpha reliability coefficient for this variable was .97. Second, self-regulatory processes include the same measures as in the analysis of the child outcomes: mastery motivation and both mother-reported and teacher-reported behavior problems measured when the child was 3 years of age.

Control Variables

Mental age. In the analysis of children's social skills, communication skills, and daily living skills, children's mental age measured at each time point was entered as a time-varying control variable.

Negative life events. In the analysis of parent well-being, a set of negative life events measured at each time point was analyzed as a time-varying control variable. The set of negative life events was based on the Life Events Scale of the PSI, which was completed independently by both mothers and fathers. The occurrence within the past year of up to five events (i.e., divorce, separation, legal problems, going into debt, and decreased income) was included in the negative life events measure. The total number of these negative life events experienced at each data collection point was calculated separately for mothers and fathers.

ANALYSIS STRATEGY

The analyses in this *Monograph* take advantage of recent developments in measuring change and identifying the predictors of change. Previously, most studies of development and adaptation have tried to measure change between two time points, using various strategies such as change scores, indexes of change, and residual change scores (Hauser-Cram & Krauss, 1991). Each of these strategies, however, is fraught with problems ranging from poor reliability, failure to account for initial status, being applicable to only certain types of measures, and being too dependent on the sample on which it is measured. Further, two time points is generally considered an inadequate basis for measuring change (Rogosa, Brand, & Zimowski, 1982).

Developments in the statistical theory of hierarchical linear models, however, facilitate the estimation of change over three or more time points based on individual growth curve analysis and enable the significant predictors of differences in those individual growth curves to be identified (Bryk & Raudenbush, 1987; Burchinal, Bailey, & Snyder, 1994; Rogosa & Willett, 1985; Willett, 1988). Further, hierarchical linear models can be designed to test hypotheses about moderators of development (Burchinal, 1999).

To apply this methodological approach to our data, we used the hierarchical linear modeling (HLM) program of Raudenbush, Bryk, Cheong, and Congdon (2000) to estimate the parameters of the hierarchical growth model. The analysis proceeded in three steps: (a) identify the basic shape of the curve for each outcome (i.e., the Level-1 or within-person model); (b) test various predictors of differences in growth (i.e., the Level-2 or between-person model); and (c) estimate growth curves for prototypical individuals to present the results.

Within-Person Models for the Child Outcomes

Within-person models estimate a growth trajectory for each individual in a sample based on the repeated measurements of a variable of interest. The repeated measures are modeled as a function of time. Depending on the function, each growth trajectory is summarized by a set of parameters. For example, the parameters that define a linear growth curve are an intercept (the point at which the origin of time is zero) and a slope (the constant rate of change per unit of time). We attempted to measure outcome variables at each of the five times of measurement described previously. As in most longitudinal studies, however, not all members in the sample participated at each time of measurement. Therefore, an individual may have provided data on an outcome measure anywhere from one to five times.

A critical feature of the computer software used in these analyses is that it allows for the estimation of individual trajectories for persons with incomplete data. To estimate an individual growth curve, HLM uses whatever information is available for an individual with incomplete data, combined with information about the parameters for the average growth trajectories for the full sample. For the child outcomes, most (69.9%) of the sample participated in all five times of measurement.

The first step in any growth analysis is to select an appropriate functional form to represent individual change over time. In setting up the within-person model, a decision needs to be made about how to center the data. The choice of centering facilitates interpretation of the intercept parameter. Centering the data involves subtracting a constant from the time scale in such a way that the point where time equals zero becomes substantively meaningful. One goal of this investigation was to identify features about children and families as they left early intervention (i.e., when the child is 3 years of age) that would predict change over time (up to age 10 years). Therefore, the within-person model was centered at age 3 years.

In order to begin to understand the shape of growth in our sample, we examined for each sample member a plot of each of the observed outcome scores versus time to see if we could determine a common pattern. The patterns appeared to be linear, and we chose to examine whether the linear function was a better fit to the data than other possible functions. Therefore, a series of growth functions were fit to the data for each outcome to assess the adequacy of their fit by examining deviance (goodness-of-fit) tests of the full model. A series of functions of time were tested on each outcome to see which model best fit the data: (a) linear, (b) quadratic, (c) log, or (d) discontinuous. Linear models were found to be the best fitting models for each of the child outcomes. The linear model is

$$Y = \beta_0 + \beta_1 * (\text{AGE} - 36) + \text{E},$$

where Y is the outcome, β_0 is the intercept or age 3 years status parameter, β_1 is the slope or rate of change parameter, 36 is age 3 years in months (where the model is centered), and E is the residual deviation of each time point from the estimated trajectory.

The next set of analyses tested whether the fit of the models could be improved by adding mental age as a time-varying covariate to the analyses of child social, communication, and daily living skills. Time-varying covariates are variables that are measured over the same time points as, and correlated with, the outcome variables. By including a time-varying covariate in the model, the time-varying influence of that variable on the outcome is controlled. For example, child mental age was the time-varying covariate tested in the analysis of change in child adaptive functioning. By controlling for mental age at each time point, the influence of mental age on growth in social, communication, and daily living skills is partialed out to get a "purer" estimation of growth in each domain. Mental age was centered on the sample mean, also called *grand mean centering.*

To check if the effect of mental age on the outcome varied by child age, we included the interaction of mental age and child age in the model. The interaction of mental age and child age was not significant in any of the models and thus was not part of the final within-person model for child social, communication, or daily living skills.

40

The final within-person model for the child adaptive functioning outcomes is

$$Y = \beta_0 + \beta_1 * (AGE - 36) + \beta_2 * (MA) + E, \qquad (1)$$

where β_2 is child mental age (MA) entered as a time-varying covariate. Table 5 provides the parameter estimates and associated standard errors for the final within-person models for each child outcome.

Children's mental age. In the final model, the age 3 status parameter is 20.70, indicating that at age 3 years the children's mental age was 20.70 months on average. Thus children are scoring well below their chronological age of 36 months. The rate of change parameter is .55, indicating that children's mental age increased, on average, by one-half (.55) month each month or 6.6 months per year (.55 * 12). There is a very high and positive correlation between the age 3 status and rate of change parameters ($r = .99$), indicating that children with a higher mental age at age 3 grow faster over time than children with lower mental ages at age 3. Finally, there is significant variation around the average growth parameters, indicating that children deviate from the mean trajectory.

TABLE 5

FINAL WITHIN-PERSON MODELS FOR CHILD OUTCOMES

Outcome	B	(SE)	df	Variance Component	χ^2
Mental age					
Age 3 status	20.698	(.70)***	182	79.490	2661.53***
Rate of change	.553	(.03)***	182	.131	7774.38***
Social skills					
Age 3 status	22.205	(.30)***	182	5.435	248.53***
Rate of change	.183	(.02)***	182	.032	352.85***
Mental age[a]	.504	(.03)***	182	.046	249.59***
Communication skills					
Age 3 status	25.101	(.35)***	182	8.994	293.72***
Rate of change	.156	(.02)***	182	.024	294.41***
Mental age[a]	.693	(.03)***	182	.039	228.60***
Daily living skills					
Age 3 status	22.835	(.33)***	182	9.831	358.64***
Rate of change	.238	(.02)***	182	.035	562.45***
Mental age[a]	.452	(.03)***	182	.039	262.24***

[a]Mental age was entered as a time-varying covariate.
***$p < .001$.

Children's social skills. In the final model (i.e., the model with mental age entered as a time-varying covariate) the age 3 status parameter indicates that children's social skills score at age 3 years, on average, was 22.20 months. Thus, as with mental age, children's scores are well below their chronological age of 36 months. The rate of change parameter indicates that children's social skills increased, on average, at a rate of .18 months per month controlling for the effect of mental age. There is a moderate and positive correlation between the age 3 status and rate of change parameters ($r = .58$), indicating that children with greater social skills at age 3 increase those skills at a faster rate than children with fewer social skills. Further, there is significant variation around the average growth parameters, indicating that children deviate substantially from the mean trajectory.

Children's communication skills. In the final model (i.e., the model with mental age entered as a time-varying covariate), the age 3 status parameter indicates that children's communication skills score at age 3 years, on average, was 25.10 months, well below their chronological age of 36 months. The rate of change parameter indicates that these skills increased, on average, at .16 months per month controlling for the effect of mental age. There is a moderate and positive correlation between the age 3 status and rate of change parameters ($r = .45$), indicating that children with higher communication skills at age 3 experience faster rates of growth in communication skills than children with lower scores. Further, there is significant variation around the average growth parameters, indicating that children deviate substantially from the mean communication skills trajectory.

Children's daily living skills. In the final model, the age 3 status parameter indicates that children's daily living skills score at age 3 years, on average, was 22.83 months, well below their chronological age of 36 months. The rate of change parameter indicates that children's daily living skills increased, on average, at .24 months per month controlling for the effect of mental age. There is a modest but positive correlation between the age 3 status and rate of change parameters ($r = .28$), indicating a weak association between children's daily living skills scores at age 3 and their rate of growth in those skills over time. Further, there is significant variation around the average growth parameters, indicating that children deviate substantially from the mean daily living skills trajectory.

Between-Person Models for the Child Outcomes

Between-person models consist of a set of simultaneous regression equations with each of the parameters estimated by the within-person model serving as outcomes or dependent variables. These equations, taken together, attempt to explain status at age 3 years and rate of change as a function of person-level predictors. In our study, the person-level predictors were measured at age 3 years because we are interested in the characteristics of children and families as they leave early intervention that predict their change over time up to age 10 years.

In creating a data set for use in the between-level analyses, HLM requires that no missing data be present. As with most studies, however, we did not have complete data for all cases for all the age 3 predictor variables that we wanted to test. Data gathered via observational and interview methodology had less missing information (0 to 15%, mean = 7%) than data gathered via questionnaires from mothers (19 to 21%, mean = 20%) and from fathers (36 to 37%, mean = 37%). After considering several strategies for data imputation (e.g., mean substitution and regression-based imputation), we chose to use the method of multiple imputation.

Multiple imputation approaches to missing data restore variability to regression-based imputations in two ways. First, based on the assumption that the residuals for the nonmissing and missing data have similar distributions, the approach restores within-imputation variability by drawing one element (randomly with replacement) from the distribution of residuals for data that are nonmissing and adding it to each imputed value. The resulting imputed data set is then available for analysis by conventional analytic methods. Second, the approach restores between-imputation variability by providing multiple estimates of the covariance matrix which is itself estimated with error. The process described above is replicated n times, providing n imputed data sets for analysis. The researcher then has n estimates of key parameters and standard errors. To obtain a reasonable point estimate of the parameter of interest one can average the multiple parameter estimates. To obtain a reasonable estimate of the standard errors, one combines the within- and between-imputation estimates of variability. New algorithms have eased the computational burden and make this approach accessible to interested researchers (Schafer, 1997).

We used Schafer's (1997) computer program NORM to conduct our analyses. In order to generate the best estimates for the missing information, variables that were not part of the conceptual models but which were correlated with the age 3 years predictor variables were included in the file used by NORM to produce the multiple estimates.

Four between-person data sets were generated by NORM and used in the construction of four sufficient statistics matrix (SSM) files in HLM. The multiple imputation function in HLM was used to analyze the four data sets and produce one "averaged" set of results. Because there is little consensus among experts as to the number of imputed data sets needed for different percentages of missing data, we experimented with different numbers of data sets to see if our results would change with more (e.g., 10) versus fewer (e.g., 4) data sets. Averaging over 10 data sets we obtained results similar to those obtained by averaging over 4 data sets, so we elected to use the smaller number of data sets.

The final HLM between-person equation for the child outcome analysis was developed based on the conceptual model depicted in Figure 1 in chapter III. All of the variables in the conceptual model were entered in one step in both the equation with status at age 3 as the outcome and the equation with the rate of change as the outcome. For the analysis of social skills, communication skills, and daily living skills, we wanted to control for the effects of mental age in all analyses. Therefore, although we allowed mental age to vary randomly across children, we were not interested in explaining that variation from person-level predictors. Building on Equation (1), the final within-person model for the child adaptive functioning outcomes, the final between-person "main effects" equations are shown below.

$$\beta_0 = G00 + G01 * (DS) + G02 * (MI) + G03 * (FEMALE) + G04 * (HEALTH)$$

$$+ G05 * (EDUC) + G06 * (MARRIED) + G07 * (MM) + G08 * (BPM)$$

$$+ G09 * (BPT) + G010 * (MC) + G011 * (FR) + \mu_0$$

$$\beta_1 = G10 + G11 * (DS) + G12 * (MI) + G13 * (FEMALE) + G14 * (HEALTH)$$

$$+ G15 * (EDUC) + G16 * (MARRIED) + G17 * (MM) + G18 * (BPM)$$

$$+ G19 * (BPT) + G110 * (MC) + G111 * (FR) + \mu_1.$$

$$\beta_2 = G20 + \mu_2,$$

where DS is the dummy variable identifying children with Down syndrome, MI is the dummy variable identifying children with motor impairment, FEMALE is the dummy variable for gender, HEALTH is the variable measuring the number of doctor visits made during the first 3 years of life, EDUC is the average of the mothers' and fathers' years of education, MARRIED is the dummy variable identifying maternal marital status, MM is the variable measuring mastery motivation, BPM is the variable measuring mother report of behavior problems, BPT is the variable measuring teacher report of behavior problems, MC is the variable measuring mother-child interaction, FR is the average of the mothers' and fathers' scores on the family relations index, and μ_0, μ_1, and μ_2 are the error terms. It is important to note that the disability group construct is fully represented by three dummy variables: DS and MI as defined above and DD for the developmentally delayed group. The DD variable is left out of the equation, thus it becomes the reference group.

Finally, a series of conceptually important interaction variables were created and entered into the analysis. Prior to creating the interaction terms, each main effect variable was centered on the sample mean to reduce the collinearity of interaction terms with the main effects (Aiken & West, 1991). The interaction term was the product of the two centered main effect variables. In the child outcome analyses, interaction terms were created for all of the following combinations of main effects: (a) child self-regulatory skills by family climate, (b) child self-regulatory skills by type of disability, (c) child self-regulatory skills by child gender, (d) family climate by type of disability, and (e) child gender by type of disability. Each interaction term was entered by itself into the final model. Only those that were statistically significant were retained in the analyses.

Within-Person Models for the Parent Outcomes

In order to study change in maternal and paternal child-related and parent-related stress, we modified our approach to incorporate the dependence of the mother-father data. At the time the children in our sample were 3 years old, more than 80% of their mothers and fathers were married (see Table 1). Using the techniques developed by Raudenbush, Brennan, and Barnett (1995), we estimated a combined model for mothers and fathers. This technique allowed us to assess how each individual in the couple was changing (differently) over time and to control for the fact that the two individual trajectories of change were likely to be related.

The model was analyzed with data from 158 couples (married or not) who were jointly raising their child with disabilities and for whom maternal and paternal outcome data had been provided on at least one occasion. Table 1 gives the basic demographic information on the full sample. In many respects, the parent subsample was not significantly different from the full sample. Similar to the full sample, the parent subsample included more children with motor impairment (36.7%) than children with Down syndrome (33.5%) or developmental delay (29.7%), and slightly more of the children were male (55.7%). Most of the sample was characterized as European American (89.2%). Almost half of the mothers (47.2%) were employed and almost all of the fathers (91.3%) were employed full-time.

The parent subsample, however, differed significantly from the full sample in expected ways. In the subsample of couples, children were more likely to live with both parents ($\chi^2(1, N = 164) = 11.68, p < .01$) and family income was higher ($\chi^2(3, N = 161) = 10.77, p < .05$). Finally, mothers were more likely to be married ($\chi^2(1, N = 161) = 10.95$, $p < .01$) in the subsample of couples than in the full sample.

Once the subsample was selected, steps similar to those utilized in the child analysis were followed. First, within-person models had to be tested to identify the appropriate functional form to represent individual change over time for both mothers and fathers. Linear models were found to be the best fitting models for maternal child-related stress and for maternal and paternal parent-related stress. The paternal child-related stress outcome, however, was best modeled with a discontinuous growth function. The discontinuous function allowed us to model a trajectory in which the increase in stress is linear at one rate of change between T1 and T3 and linear at a different rate of change between T3 and T5. Therefore, different equations were needed to model child-related stress and parent-related stress. The linear model for parent-related stress is:

$$Y = (\text{mother})[\beta_1 + \beta_2 * (\text{AGE} - 36) + E]$$

$$+ (\text{father})[\beta_3 + \beta_4 * (\text{AGE} - 36) + E], \qquad (2)$$

where Y is the outcome, mother is a dummy variable identifying maternal data, β_1 is the intercept or age 3 status parameter for the mother equation, β_2 is the slope or rate of change parameter for the mother equation, father is a dummy variable identifying paternal data, β_3 is the intercept or age 3 status parameter for the father equation, β_4 is the slope or rate of change parameter for the father equation, and E is the residual deviation of each time point from the estimated trajectory.

The child-related stress model, presented in Equation (3), includes a parameter in the paternal model that describes the increment or decrement to the paternal linear baseline rate. We define this parameter as the discontinuous term.

$$Y = (\text{mother})[\beta_1 + \beta_2 * (\text{AGE} - 36) + E]$$

$$+ (\text{father})[\beta_3 + \beta_4 * (\text{AGE} - 36) + \beta_5 * (\text{DISC}) + E], \qquad (3)$$

where β_5 is the discontinuous term (i.e., the increment or decrement to the baseline rate beginning at age T3) for the father equation.

The next set of analyses tested whether the fit of the models could be improved by adding time-varying covariates. We tested negative life events as a time-varying covariate to control for the influence at each time point that other life experiences (e.g., going into debt, divorce or separation, legal problems) may have had on stress related to the child or related to the parental role. In addition, we tested whether the effect of negative life events varied by the child's age by including an interaction term of negative life events and child's age.

Negative life events proved to be significant in the equations modeling maternal child-related stress and maternal and paternal parent-related stress. Thus, building on Equation (2), the final within-person model for parent-related stress is

$$Y = (\text{mother})[\beta_1 + \beta_2 * (\text{AGE} - 36) + \beta_3 * (\text{MNLE}) + E]$$

$$+ (\text{father})[\beta_4 + \beta_5 * (\text{AGE} - 36) + \beta_6 * (\text{FNLE}) + E], \qquad (4)$$

where β_3 is maternal report of negative life events (MNLE) entered as a time-varying covariate in the mother equation, and β_6 is paternal report of negative life events (FNLE) entered as a time varying covariate in the father equation.

The final within-person model for child-related stress (building on Equation 3) is:

$$Y = (\text{mother})[\beta_1 + \beta_2 * (\text{AGE} - 36)\ \beta_3 * (\text{MNLE}) + E]$$

$$+ (\text{father})\ [\beta_4 + \beta_5 * (\text{AGE} - 36) + \beta_6 * (\text{DISC}) + E]. \qquad (5)$$

The parameter estimates and associated standard errors for the within-person models are presented in Table 6.

Maternal and paternal child-related stress. The mean trajectories of child-related stress for mothers and fathers are presented in Figure 3. Child-related stress increased for both mothers and fathers over the entire range of the observation period. The increase for mothers was linear, and child-related stress for fathers increased at one rate between entry to early intervention and the child reaching age 3 years and at a lower, but still positive, rate between age 3 years and age 10 years. The average paternal child-related stress scores were somewhat higher than the maternal scores at each point of measurement except at age 10. In fact, comparisons between the intercept or age 3 status parameters found that the paternal child-related stress score at age 3 years ($M = 112.62$) was significantly greater than the maternal child-related stress score at age 3 ($M = 106.99$, $\chi^2(1, N = 157) = 11.85$, $p < .001$). The overall average rate of increase in paternal child-related stress ($M = .17$ points per month), however, was not significantly greater than the average overall rate of increase in maternal child-related stress ($M = .13$ points per month, $\chi^2(1, N = 157) = 0.49$, $p > .05$). The coefficient on the discontinuous term in the father equation was $-.11$, indicating that there was a decrement to the rate of increase in paternal child-related stress after the child was 3 years old. The rate of increase after age 3 was .06 (i.e., $.17 - .11 = .06$). When their child was

TABLE 6

FINAL WITHIN-PERSON MODELS FOR PARENT OUTCOMES

Outcome	B	(SE)	df	Variance Component	χ^2
Child-related stress					
Mother age 3 status	106.988	(1.36)***	157	255.497	666.11***
Mother rate of change	.134	(.02)***	157	.041	217.39***
Mother NLE[a]	2.029	(.92)*	157	42.912	166.31***
Father age 3 status	112.617	(1.82)***	157	401.659	379.83***
Father rate of change	.172	(.06)**	157	.217	149.03***
Father disc[b]	−.114	(.07)	157	.252	118.44***
Parent-related stress					
Mother age 3 status	119.445	(1.75)***	157	433.687	807.60***
Mother rate of change	.045	(.02)*	157	.034	161.75***
Mother NLE[a]	4.131	(.97)***	157	46.175	140.71***
Father age 3 status	117.245	(1.59)***	157	326.701	460.15***
Father rate of change	.082	(.02)***	157	.033	136.56***
Father NLE[a]	3.625	(1.27)**	157	87.983	131.97***

[a]Mother and father reports of negative life events (NLE) were entered as time-varying covariates.
[b]Disc = Discontinuous term.
*$p < .05$; **$p < .01$; ***$p < .001$.

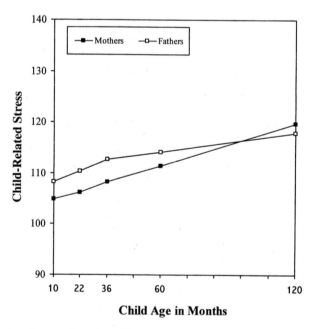

FIGURE 3.—Mean trajectories of maternal and paternal child-related stress.

48

10 years old, the increase in stress for both parents resulted in 38.1% of mothers and 43.7% of fathers reporting scores in the clinical referral range (indicated by a cutoff score that would be expected for 10% of the population).

There was a high correlation between the maternal and paternal linear rates of change ($r = .64$). Finally, there is significant variation around the average growth parameters indicating that both mothers and fathers deviate substantially from their mean child-related stress trajectories.

Maternal and paternal parent-related stress. The mean trajectories of parent-related stress for mothers and fathers are presented in Figure 4. Comparisons between the status parameters found that although the maternal parent-related stress score at age 3 years ($M = 119.44$) was somewhat higher than the paternal parent-related stress score ($M = 117.24$), the difference was not statistically significant ($\chi^2(1, N = 157) = 1.45$, $p > .05$). Although the increase in paternal parent-related stress was greater ($M = .08$) than the increase in maternal parent-related stress ($M = .04$), the rates of change were not significantly different ($\chi^2(1, N = 157) = 2.13$, $p > .05$). Mother and father parent-related stress scores were nearly equivalent at age 10

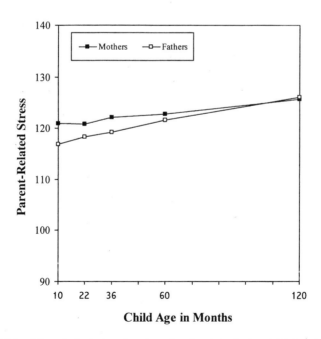

FIGURE 4.—Mean trajectories of maternal and paternal parent-related stress.

years. In contrast to the findings for child-related stress, however, few mothers (11.4%) and few fathers (10.7%) scored above the cutoff level for clinical referral when their child was age 10. Also in comparison to the child-related stress findings, there was a more modest correlation between the maternal and paternal parent-related stress trajectories ($r = .37$).

Between-Person Models for the Parent Outcomes

Similar to the between-person models for the child outcomes, the between-person models for the parent outcomes consisted of a set of simultaneous regression equations with each of the parameters estimated by the within-person model serving as outcomes or dependent variables. As described earlier, the parameters for the within-person models for both the child-related and parent-related stress outcomes included status at age 3 years and rate of change. The model for child-related stress also included a discontinuous term as a parameter. The final HLM between-person equation for the parent outcome analysis was developed based on the conceptual model depicted in Figure 2 in this chapter. All of the variables in the conceptual model were entered in one step in the equations with status at age 3 as the outcome, the equations with the rate of change as the outcome, and the equation with the discontinuous term as the outcome. The analysis of both parent outcomes also controlled for the effects of negative life events. Although we allowed negative life events to vary randomly across mothers and fathers, we were not interested in explaining that variation from person-level predictors. Therefore, building on the final within-person model for child-related stress presented in Equation (5), the final between-person main effects equations for child-related stress are as follows:

$$\beta_1 = G10 + G11 * (DS) + G12 * (MI) + G13 * (FEMALE) + G14 * (HEALTH)$$
$$+ G15 * (MED) + G16 * (MMAR) + G17 * (MM) + G18 * (IQ)$$
$$+ G19 * (ADAP) + G110 * (MC) + G111 * (MFR) + G112 * (MSS)$$
$$+ G113 * (MPFC) + G114 * (BPM) + G115 * (BPT) + \mu_1$$

$$\beta_2 = G20 + G21 * (DS) + G22 * (MI) + G23 * (FEMALE) + G24 * (HEALTH)$$
$$+ G25 * (MED) + G26 * (MMAR) + G27 * (MM) + G28 * (IQ)$$
$$+ G29 * (ADAP) + G210 * (MC) + G211 * (MFR) + G212 * (MSS)$$
$$+ G213 * (MPFC) + G214 * (BPM) + G215 * (BPT) + \mu_2$$

$$\beta_3 = G30 + \mu_3$$

$$\beta_4 = G40 + G41 * (DS) + G42 * (MI) + G43 * (FEMALE) + G44 * (HEALTH)$$
$$+ G45 * (FED) + G46 * (FMAR) + G47 * (MM) + G48 * (IQ)$$
$$+ G49 * (ADAP) + G410 * (MC) + G411 * (FFR) + G412 * (FSS)$$
$$+ G413 * (FPFC) + G414 * (BPM) + G415 * (BPT) + \mu_4$$

$$\beta_5 = G50 + G51 * (DS) + G52 * (MI) + G53 * (FEMALE) + G54 * (HEALTH)$$
$$+ G55 * (FED) + G56 * (FMAR) + G57 * (MM) + G58 * (IQ)$$
$$+ G59 * (ADAP) + G510 * (MC) + G511 * (FFR) + G512 * (FSS)$$
$$+ G513 * (FPFC) + G514 * (BPM) + G515 * (BPT) + \mu_5$$

$$\beta_6 = G60 + G61 * (DS) + G62 * (MI) + G63 * (FEMALE) + G64 * (HEALTH)$$
$$+ G65 * (FED) + G66 * (FMAR) + G67 * (MM) + G68 * (IQ)$$
$$+ G69 * (ADAP) + G610 * (MC) + G611 * (FFR) + G612 * (FSS)$$
$$+ G613 * (FPFC) + G614 * (BPM) + G615 * (BPT) + \mu_6,$$

where DS is the dummy variable identifying children with Down syndrome, MI is the dummy variable identifying children with motor impairment, FEMALE is the dummy variable for gender, HEALTH is the variable measuring the number of doctor visits made during the first 3 years of life, MED is mothers' and FED is fathers' years of education, MMAR and FMAR are the dummy variables identifying maternal and paternal marital status, MM is the variable measuring mastery motivation, IQ is the variable measuring child cognitive skills, ADAP is the variable measuring child adaptive skills, MC is the variable measuring mother-child interaction, MFR and FFR are the variables measuring mother and father family relations, MSS and FSS are the variables measuring mother and father social support, MPFC and FPFC are the variables measuring mother and father problem-focused coping, BPM is the variable measuring mother report of behavior problems, BPT is the variable measuring teacher report of behavior problems, and μ_1, μ_2, μ_3, μ_4, μ_5, and μ_6 are the error terms.

The final between-person main effects equations for parent-related stress are similar to the child-related stress models except that there is no discontinuous term. Instead, both maternal and paternal negative life events are entered as time-varying covariates. As such, they are allowed to vary randomly but are not predicted from person-level predictors. Thus, building on the final within-person model for parent-related stress presented in Equation (4), the final between-person main effects equations for parent-related stress are as follows:

$$\beta_1 = G10 + G11 * (DS) + G12 * (MI) + G13 * (FEMALE) + G14 * (HEALTH)$$
$$+ G15 * (MED) + G16 * (MMAR) + G17 * (MM) + G18 * (IQ)$$
$$+ G19 * (ADAP) + G110 * (MC) + G111 * (MFR) + G112 * (MSS)$$
$$+ G113 * (MPFC) + G114 * (BPM) + G115 * (BPT) + \mu_1$$

$$\beta_2 = G20 + G21 * (DS) + G22 * (MI) + G23 * (FEMALE) + G24 * (HEALTH)$$
$$+ G25 * (MED) + G26 * (MMAR) + G27 * (MM) + G28 * (IQ)$$
$$+ G29 * (ADAP) + G210 * (MC) + G211 * (MFR) + G212 * (MSS)$$
$$+ G213 * (MPFC) + G214 * (BPM) + G215 * (BPT) + \mu_2$$

$$\beta_3 = G30 + \mu_3$$

$$\beta_4 = G40 + G41 * (DS) + G42 * (MI) + G43 * (FEMALE) + G44 * (HEALTH)$$
$$+ G45 * (FED) + G46 * (FMAR) + G47 * (MM) + G48 * (IQ)$$
$$+ G49 * (ADAP) + G410 * (MC) + G411 * (FFR) + G412 * (FSS)$$
$$+ G413 * (FPFC) + G414 * (BPM) + G415 * (BPT) + \mu_4$$

$$\beta_5 = G50 + G51 * (DS) + G52 * (MI) + G53 * (FEMALE) + G54 * (HEALTH)$$
$$+ G55 * (FED) + G56 * (FMAR) + G57 * (MM) + G58 * (IQ)$$
$$+ G59 * (ADAP) + G510 * (MC) + G511 * (FFR) + G512 * (FSS)$$
$$+ G513 * (FPFC) + G514 * (BPM) + G515 * (BPT) + \mu_5$$

$$\beta_6 = G60 + \mu_6.$$

In addition to all of the main effects models, we tested for interaction effects by entering selected interaction terms, one at a time, in each model. The interaction effects we tested for were the same as those we examined in the child outcome analysis. In addition, however, interactions between child development skills (e.g., cognitive and adaptive skills) and family climate, type of disability, and child gender were also examined. Only the significant interaction effects are reported in the results described in the next chapter (see chapter IV).

Finally, we conducted a series of analyses where we entered maternal reported variables (e.g., mothers' family relations index score) as predictors of both paternal stress measures and we entered paternal reported variables (e.g., fathers' family relations index score) as predictors of both maternal stress measures. This was done to further examine the influence of individuals on their partners. None of these "partner predictor variables" was significant and thus none are reported in chapter IV.

Presentation of Results for Child and Parent Outcomes

In order to highlight the significant findings, a series of graphs were produced that summarize the fitted relationships between change in each outcome and the significant predictors of interest. Therefore, the figures presented in chapter IV present the growth curves of "prototypical" individuals. These are individuals who have specific values for a selected significant predictor variable or for a selected set of predictor variables and sample mean values for the other predictor variables in the model. Thus, these growth curves are designed to show the effect of a selected significant variable or variables on change over time in a specified outcome. The "Hi" and "Lo" designations on the graphs indicate trajectories for prototypical individuals with scores on the variable of interest that are 1.5 standard deviations above and below the sample mean.

IV. RESULTS: PREDICTORS OF FUNCTIONING
AND CHANGE IN CHILDREN'S DEVELOPMENT
AND PARENT WELL-BEING

The analyses were designed to test the extent to which children's development is related to their own self-regulatory behavior and their family climate. We also tested the extent to which family and child characteristics are related to changes in the well-being of both mothers and fathers.

As described in chapter III, we developed a series of graphic displays of the growth curves of "prototypical" children or parents to depict the effects of significant between-person predictors, as measured at age 3 years, on change over time in each of the outcomes. The gap between the growth curves on each graph represents the magnitude of the effect of a specific predictor variable on the outcome, net of the other variables in the equation (the other variables are set at the average value). Further, the trajectories are shown over the mean child age at each time of measurement. In the following sections we describe the predictors of functioning and change in children's cognitive and adaptive development and in parent well-being.

The tables in this chapter, which present the findings for the analysis of child outcomes, use the symbol β_0 to represent the latent variables for status or functioning at age 3 years and the symbol β_1 to represent the latent variable for rate of growth. Similarly, the tables that present the findings for the analysis of parent outcomes use β_1 to represent the latent variable for maternal functioning at age 3, β_2 to represent the latent variable for maternal rate of change, β_4 to represent the latent variable for paternal functioning at age 3, and β_5 to represent the latent variable for paternal rate of change. The table that presents the findings for child-related stress also uses the symbol β_6 to represent the latent variable for the paternal discontinuous function (see chapter III). Each latent variable is an outcome or dependent variable in the between-person models and is predicted by age 3 predictor variables.

CHILDREN'S MENTAL AGE AND ADAPTIVE BEHAVIOR

Both mental age and adaptive behavior were selected as outcomes for children because of their importance for both school and life skills (Harrison, 1987). To facilitate interpretation, these outcomes were analyzed as age equivalence scores (in months) rather than as standardized scores. Further, age equivalence scores have a growth function and therefore meet a requirement for growth modeling.

As described in chapter III, a within-person model was fit for each outcome. A linear model was the best descriptor of change in all outcomes. For analyses of the conceptual models for adaptive behavior (described in Figure 1), we developed within-person models that included mental age as a time-varying covariate because its inclusion improved the model. The term for the time-varying covariate was significant for each of the adaptive behavior outcomes. This indicates that including mental age as time-varying (instead of time invariant) better captures its effect and ensures more precise estimation of the standard errors. This approach also reveals the relation of hypothesized predictors to each aspect of adaptive behavior beyond the "effect" of cognition. Thus, the between-person variables that are significant correlates of level of functioning at age 3 years and significant predictors of change in adaptive behavior (presented in the final models) are those that account for significant additional variance beyond that predicted by changes in children's mental age. The final models contained all hypothesized variables, and the results reported are those that were significant net of the effect of other variables.

Mental Age

At age 3 years, children with higher mastery motivation scores also demonstrated higher mental age scores at age 3 (see Table 7). The effect of the interaction of type of disability by mastery motivation on the age 3 status parameter, however, indicates that the relation between mastery motivation and mental age, which is strong for children with motor impairment and developmental delay, is weaker for children with Down syndrome. Children whose mothers had higher scores on the measure of mother-child interaction when the child was age 3 also had higher mental age scores at age 3, but this effect was moderated by the child's disability group; the effect was weaker for children with Down syndrome in comparison to children in the other two groups. Finally, mothers reported more, and teachers fewer, child behavior problems for children with higher mental age scores at age 3 years, and these relations did not vary by type of disability.

Neither child nor parent demographic characteristics predicted change in children's mental age over the 10-year period. Child self-regulatory

TABLE 7

GROWTH CURVE ANALYSIS: PREDICTING TRAJECTORIES OF
DEVELOPMENT IN MENTAL AGE

	β_0 (SE) (age 3 status)		β_1 (SE) (rate of change)	
		Final Model		
Intercepts	2.891	(7.01)	−.037	(.29)
Child characteristics				
Type of disability[a]				
Down syndrome (DS)	15.029	(7.67)	.520	(.32)
Motor impairment (MI)	11.305	(10.87)	.516	(.43)
Gender (female)	.471	(1.15)	.009	(.05)
Health	−.024	(.03)	−.001	(.00)
Parent characteristics				
Years of education	.135	(.24)	−.003	(.01)
Marital status (married)	.099	(1.60)	.039	(.06)
Child self-regulatory processes				
Mastery motivation (MM)	2.381	(.82)*	.095	(.03)**
Behavior problems (mother)	1.400	(.64)*	.043	(.02)
Behavior problems (teacher)	−1.094	(.48)*	−.048	(.02)*
Family climate				
Mother-child interaction (MC)	.593	(.18)**	.023	(.01)**
Family relations	−.298	(.23)	−.012	(.01)
Interaction terms				
DS × MM	−2.065	(.87)*	−.091	(.03)**
MI × MM	.585	(1.13)	.016	(.04)
DS × MC	−.549	(.20)**	−.020	(.01)*
MI × MC	−.389	(.29)	−.017	(.01)

[a]Children with developmental delay are the reference group.
*$p < .05$; **$p < .01$.

behaviors and the family climate were predictors of change in mental age, however. Two aspects of children's self-regulatory behavior, behavior problems and mastery motivation, predicted change in children's cognitive skills. Children whose teachers rated them as having higher levels of behavior problems at age 3 years demonstrated less growth in mental age (see Figure 5). Children with higher mastery motivation demonstrated more growth in mental age, but the interaction term for type of disability by mastery motivation was also significant. As can be seen in Figure 6, children with high levels of mastery motivation in each of the three disability groups outperformed those with low levels. This difference was most prominent for children with motor impairment and developmental delay, and considerably less so for children with Down syndrome.

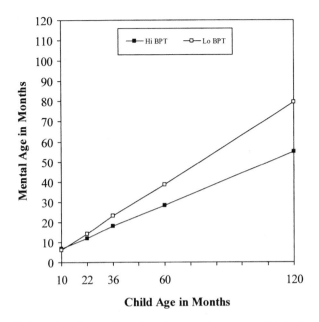

FIGURE 5.—Trajectories of mental age based on teacher report of behavior problems.

One aspect of the family climate, mother-child interaction, predicted greater change in mental age (see Figure 7). This result is qualified, however, by an interaction between mother-child interaction and type of disability. Although children whose mothers had more positive interactive skills demonstrated greater growth in mental age over time, these differences were most pronounced for children with either motor impairment or developmental delay. Thus, the interaction terms for both mastery motivation and mother-child interaction suggest that the relation between these processes and growth in child mental age was weaker for children with Down syndrome than for children with other disabilities.

Adaptive Behavior

In analyzing adaptive behavior, we examined correlates of children's functioning at age 3 years and predictors of change over the study period. Three domains of the Vineland scales were analyzed: social, communication, and daily living. In the final models we controlled for mental age over time to predict changes in adaptive behavior beyond the contribution of cognition. We also tested for possible interaction terms in these models, but we found no interactions to be significant. Additionally, we

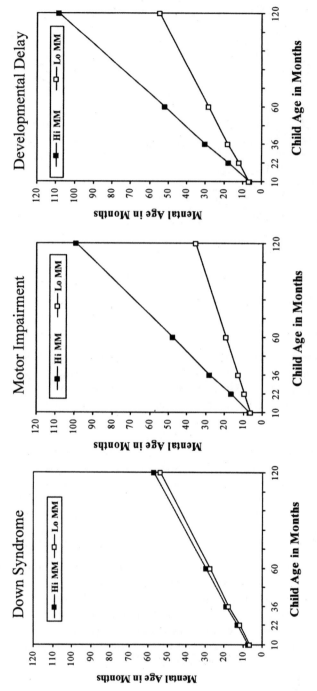

Figure 6.— Trajectories of mental age based on mastery motivation by type of disability.

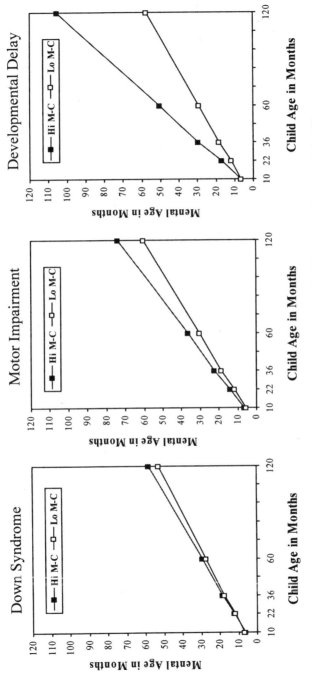

FIGURE 7.—Trajectories of mental age based on mother-child interaction by type of disability.

examined two sets of final models, one with and one without mental age as a time-varying covariate. In keeping with the approach recommended by Baron and Kenny (1986), we made comparisons of the parameter estimates to determine if mental age mediates the relation between the tested predictors and the adaptive behavior outcomes. We found that the coefficients were reduced in the final models for communication skills and daily living skills, suggesting that mental age is a partial (but not full) mediator of children's adaptive behavior skills in those domains.

Social skills. When mental age was controlled, no other variables were significantly related to the child's social skills functioning at age 3 years (see Table 8). In relation to change in social skills, children with Down syndrome in comparison to those with motor impairment or developmental delay, had greater change in the development of social skills. Both

TABLE 8

GROWTH CURVE ANALYSIS: PREDICTING TRAJECTORIES OF
DEVELOPMENT IN SOCIAL SKILLS[a,b]

	Final Model		
	β_0 (*SE*) (age 3 status)	β_1 (*SE*) (rate of change)	B_2 (*SE*) (control)
Intercepts	20.073 (2.49)***	.023 (.11)	.488 (.04)***
Child characteristics			
Type of disability[c]			
Down syndrome	.298 (.71)	.060 (.03)*	
Motor impairment	.195 (.72)	.026 (.03)	
Gender (female)	−.206 (.54)	−.029 (.02)	
Health	−.029 (.02)	−.000 (.00)	
Parent characteristics			
Years of education	−.110 (.13)	−.009 (.00)	
Marital status (married)	−.253 (.70)	.014 (.03)	
Child self-regulatory processes			
Mastery motivation	.223 (.20)	.012 (.01)	
Behavior problems (mother)	−.270 (.30)	−.006 (.01)	
Behavior problems (teacher)	−.335 (.20)	−.011 (.01)	
Family climate			
Mother-child interaction	.086 (.05)	.004 (.00)*	
Family relations	.130 (.12)	.011 (.00)*	

[a]Controlling for mental age as a time-varying covariate.
[b]No interaction terms were significant.
[c]Children with developmental delay are the reference group.
*$p < .05$; ***$p < .001$.

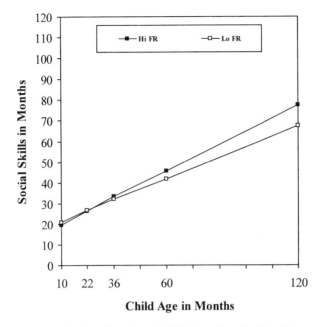

FIGURE 8.—Trajectories of social skills based on family relations.

aspects of the family climate were predictive of changes in social skills. Mothers with higher mother-child interaction scores and families with more positively rated family relations had children who showed greater positive change in social skills. In fact, family relations was the most potent of the three significant predictors of change in social skills (see Figure 8), as children from families with stronger (in comparison to weaker) relations demonstrated approximately a 10-month advantage in social skills by age 10 years.

Communication skills. When mental age was controlled, mother-child interaction was the only significant correlate of communication skills at age 3 years (see Table 9). Mother-child interaction was also the only construct that predicted change in communication skills; mothers with higher levels of interactive skills had children who made greater changes in their communication skills beyond those predicted by changes in mental age (see Figure 9). By 10 years of age, children whose mothers had more positive (in comparison to those with less positive) mother-child interaction skills demonstrated approximately a 10-month advantage in communication skills.

61

TABLE 9

GROWTH CURVE ANALYSIS: PREDICTING TRAJECTORIES OF
DEVELOPMENT IN COMMUNICATION SKILLS[a,b]

	Final Model		
	β_0 (SE) (age 3 status)	β_1 (SE) (rate of change)	B_2 (SE) (control)
Intercepts	22.643 (2.72)***	.054 (.10)	.641 (.04)***
Child characteristics			
Type of disability[c]			
Down syndrome	−1.294 (.82)	−.006 (.03)	
Motor impairment	.359 (.91)	.008 (.03)	
Gender (female)	−.064 (.61)	.003 (.02)	
Health	−.026 (.02)	−.000 (.00)	
Parent characteristics			
Years of education	−.164 (.14)	−.006 (.00)	
Marital status (married)	−.197 (.92)	−.005 (.03)	
Child self-regulatory processes			
Mastery motivation	.310 (.25)	.011 (.01)	
Behavior problems (mother)	−.239 (.38)	−.002 (.01)	
Behavior problems (teacher)	−.424 (.25)	−.016 (.01)	
Family climate			
Mother-child interaction	.121 (.06)*	.005 (.00)*	
Family relations	.111 (.14)	.004 (.00)	

[a]Controlling for mental age as a time-varying covariate.
[b]No interaction terms were significant.
[c]Children with developmental delay are the reference group.
*$p < .05$; ***$p < .001$.

Daily living skills. When mental age was controlled, only one variable, parent education, was a significant correlate of children's functioning in daily living skills at age 3 years (see Table 10). In terms of growth in daily living skills, children with motor impairment had less growth than children in the other two disability groups. Also, children who had higher levels of mastery motivation at age 3 showed greater growth in the acquisition of daily living skills over time (see Figure 10). Children with stronger (in comparison to those with weaker) levels of mastery motivation demonstrated daily living skills that were approximately 14 months higher by age 10 years.

Summary of Findings for Children's Development

Differences by type of disability were found for several of the outcomes studied. For children with motor impairment or developmental

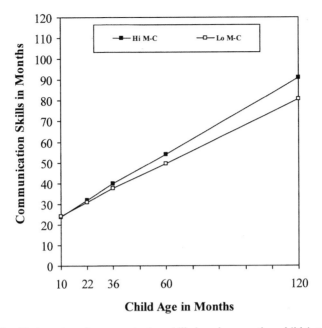

FIGURE 9.—Trajectories of communication skills based on mother-child interaction.

delay, growth in mental age was related to both their own mastery motivation and their mother's interactive skills; these relations were weaker for children with Down syndrome. Children with Down syndrome, however, demonstrated comparatively greater growth in social skills, whereas children with motor impairment had less growth in daily living skills (see Table 11).

Regardless of type of disability, children with fewer teacher-reported behavior problems at age 3 years made greater gains in mental age. Changes in children's mental age correlated positively with changes in all three adaptive behavior outcomes. Other variables, however, also predicted change in child adaptive functioning. One child self-regulatory process, mastery motivation, predicted growth in daily living skills. Two features of the family climate predicted change in domains of child adaptive functioning. Mother-child interaction predicted change in both communication skills and social skills. Family relations also predicted change in social skills. These findings suggest the important and complex relations among child self-regulatory processes, the family climate, and children's development.

TABLE 10

GROWTH CURVE ANALYSIS: PREDICTING TRAJECTORIES OF DEVELOPMENT IN DAILY LIVING SKILLS[a,b]

| | Final Model | | |
	β_0 (SE) (age 3 status)	β_1 (SE) (rate of change)	B_2 (SE) (control)
Intercepts	26.820 (2.50)***	.306 (.10)**	.424 (.03)***
Child characteristics			
Type of disability[c]			
Down syndrome	−1.264 (.68)	−.040 (.03)	
Motor impairment	−1.039 (.75)	−.079 (.03)*	
Gender (female)	.006 (.55)	.013 (.02)	
Health	−.023 (.02)	−.000 (.00)	
Parent characteristics			
Years of education	−.346 (.12)**	−.010 (.00)	
Marital status (married)	−.487 (.88)	−.006 (.03)	
Child self-regulatory processes			
Mastery motivation	.276 (.19)	.030 (.01)**	
Behavior problems (mother)	−.560 (.33)	−.016 (.01)	
Behavior problems (teacher)	−.180 (.20)	−.003 (.01)	
Family climate			
Mother-child interaction	.069 (.05)	.004 (.00)	
Family relations	.007 (.14)	−.001 (.00)	

[a]Controlling for mental age as a time-varying covariate.
[b]No interaction terms were significant.
[c]Children with developmental delay are the reference group.
*p < .05; **p < .01; ***p < .001.

TABLE 11

SUMMARY OF SIGNIFICANT PREDICTORS OF CHANGE IN CHILDREN'S DEVELOPMENT

Outcome	Main Effects[a] (slope)	Interactions[a] (slope)
Mental age	Mastery motivation (MM) Mother-child interaction (MC) Behavior problems (T)	DS × MM DS × MC
Social skills	Down syndrome (DS) Mother-child interaction Mother/father family relations	None
Communication skills	Mother-child interaction	None
Daily living skills	Motor impairment Mastery motivation	None

[a]MM = mastery motivation, DS = Down syndrome, MC = mother-child interaction, T = teacher report.

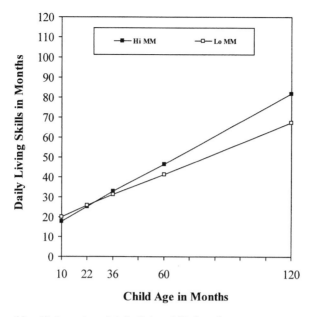

FIGURE 10.—Trajectories of daily living skills based on mastery motivation.

PARENT WELL-BEING

Child-related and parent-related stress were selected as measures of well-being for both mothers and fathers. As discussed in chapter III, two within-person models were estimated, one for maternal and paternal child-related stress and one for maternal and paternal parent-related stress. Models combining mother and father data on the same outcome were estimated (as opposed to analyzing separate models for each parent) to account for the high correlation between partners' trajectories of stress. In addition, the final models contained all hypothesized variables, and the results reported are those that were significant net of the effect of other variables.

Maternal and Paternal Child-Related Stress

Four child characteristic variables were significant correlates of maternal child-related stress at age 3 years (see Table 12). Mothers of children with Down syndrome and mothers of children with motor impairment experienced less child-related stress than did mothers of children with

TABLE 12

GROWTH CURVE ANALYSIS: PREDICTING TRAJECTORIES OF CHANGE IN CHILD-RELATED STRESS[a]

	Final Model					
	Maternal			Paternal		
	β_1 (SE) (age 3 status)	β_2 (SE) (rate of change)	β_3[b] (SE) (control)	β_4 (SE) (age 3 status)	β_5 (SE) (rate of change)	β_6[c] (disc) (SE)
Intercepts	132.778 (28.83)***	.254 (.18)	1.107 (1.00)	147.850 (16.31)	1.366 (.53)	-1.279 (.63)*
Child characteristics						
Type of disability[d]						
Down syndrome	-5.857 (2.69)*	.097 (.04)*		-3.335 (4.56)	-.079 (.16)	.095 (.20)
Motor impairment	-6.900 (2.67)*	-.029 (.05)		-2.746 (4.07)	-.023 (.16)	-.050 (.19)
Gender (female)	1.364 (2.06)	-.018 (.04)		4.181 (3.44)	.259 (.12)*	-.337 (.15)*
Health	.071 (.10)	.000 (.00)		.064 (.14)	-.002 (.00)	.000 (.01)
Parent characteristics						
Years of education	.042 (.43)	.009 (.01)		1.125 (.53)*	.018 (.02)	-.031 (.02)
Marital status (married)	5.318 (2.81)	-.052 (.05)		2.458 (5.50)	-.176 (.19)	.207 (.24)
Parenting assets						
Problem-focused coping	-6.281 (10.87)	-.349 (.21)		-5.226 (18.68)	-.249 (.65)	-.011 (.84)
Support helpfulness	-.131 (.13)	-.002 (.00)		-.172 (.70)	-.010 (.01)	.010 (.01)
Family climate						
Mother-child interaction	.057 (.19)	.001 (.00)		-.561 (.28)*	-.017 (.01)	.025 (.01)*
Family relations	-.569 (.37)	-.001 (.01)		-.541 (.53)	-.009 (.02)	.012 (.02)
Child development skills						
Cognitive skills	-.033 (.08)	-.001 (.00)		-.185 (.12)	-.006 (.01)	.005 (.01)
Adaptive skills	-.771 (.25)**	.002 (.00)		-.453 (.37)	.012 (.02)	-.008 (.02)
Child self-regulatory processes						
Mastery motivation	1.721 (.81)*	-.023 (.01)		1.030 (1.07)	-.042 (.04)	.036 (.05)
Behavior problems (mother)	7.524 (1.45)***	.054 (.02)*		7.022 (1.66)***	.168 (.06)**	-.160 (.07)*
Behavior problems (teacher)	-.676 (.81)	.034 (.01)**		1.172 (1.29)	.034 (.04)	-.023 (.05)

[a]No interaction terms were significant.
[b]Controlling for maternal report of negative life events as a time-varying covariate.
[c]Disc = Discontinuous term.
[d]Children with developmental delay are the reference group.
*p .05; **p < .01; ***p < .001.

developmental delay. Mothers of children with more behavior problems and (surprisingly) greater mastery motivation skills reported greater child-related stress when the child was 3 years of age. In contrast, mothers of children with higher adaptive behavior skills reported less child-related stress. Finally, no parent demographics or family climate variables were significant correlates of maternal child-related stress.

Similar to the findings for mothers, higher paternal child-related stress at age 3 years was correlated with children's higher behavior problem scores. In contrast, fathers with more years of education also reported significantly higher levels of child-related stress when their child was 3 years of age. Lower paternal child-related stress at age 3 was also correlated with higher mother-child interaction but was unaffected by child disability group, child mastery motivation skills, and child adaptive behavior skills.

As shown in chapter III, although both maternal and paternal child-related stress increased between entry to early intervention and age 10 years, the patterns of increase were different. Mothers' child-related stress increased linearly at an average rate of .13 points per month throughout the entire early to middle childhood period. In contrast, fathers' child-related stress was best modeled with a discontinuous growth function that enabled us to predict the overall rate of change (the slope) as well as the decrement to the baseline rate beginning at age 3 (the discontinuous term). For fathers, child-related stress increased linearly at an average rate of .17 points per month between entry to early intervention and age 3 years and then continued to increase linearly from age 3 to age 10 years but at a much lower rate (.06 points per month). In addition, the analysis of maternal, but not paternal, child-related stress controlled for the significant influence of negative life events. (The measure of life events was not a significant term in modeling fathers' child-related stress.) Although both child and family characteristics were significant predictors of these increases, different factors accounted for change in maternal versus paternal child-related stress.

The one common significant predictor of change for both mothers and fathers was mother-reported child behavior problems. Figure 11 compares the trajectories for parents of children with higher and lower behavior problem scores. Mothers of children with higher behavior problem scores experienced a significant increase in child-related stress; in contrast, the child-related stress scores for mothers of children with lower behavior problem scores remained fairly stable, and low, over time. The difference in these trajectories demonstrates the significant relation between behavior problems and change in maternal child-related stress.

Mother-reported child behavior problems also influenced the overall rate of change (the slope) and the decrement to the overall rate of change in child-related stress experienced by fathers from the time their child

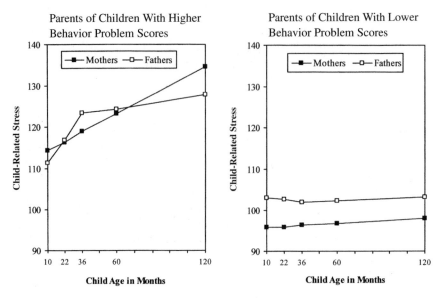

FIGURE 11.—Trajectories of maternal and paternal child-related stress based on mother report of child behavior problems.

was age 3 years to age 10 years (the discontinuous term). Fathers of children with higher behavior problem scores experienced a steep increase in child-related stress between entry to early intervention and age 3 and continuing increases in stress, but at a much lower rate, between ages 3 and 10 years. In contrast, fathers of children with lower behavior problem scores reported low and slightly decreasing child-related stress scores between entry to early intervention and age 3 and then slight increases in stress from age 3 to age 10. At all time points, the child-related stress scores for fathers of children with lower behavior problems were much lower than for fathers of children with higher behavior problems.

A formal test was conducted to compare the maternal and paternal slope parameters associated with mother-reported behavior problems because that was the only common significant predictor of change in child-related stress. No significant difference (χ^2 (1, $N = 158$) = 3.05, $p > .05$) was found between the predictive power of behavior problems on change in mother versus father child-related stress.

Behavior problems reported by the child's preschool teacher were also examined as a predictor of change in child-related stress for mothers and fathers. For mothers, teacher-reported behavior problems was a significant predictor of change in child-related stress, controlling for mother-reported behavior problems. Given the problem of shared variance between

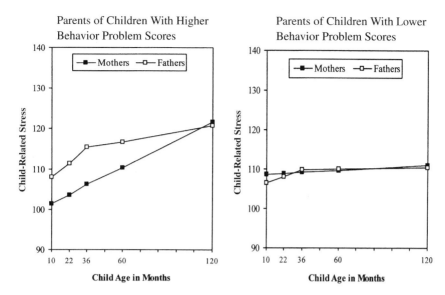

FIGURE 12.—Trajectories of maternal and paternal child-related stress based on teacher report of child behavior problems.

maternal reports of child behavior problems and child-related stress, finding that an independent measure of child behavior problems also predicts change in maternal child-related stress is important.

The trajectories of child-related stress for parents of children with higher and lower behavior problem scores as reported by the children's teachers can be seen in Figure 12. Mothers of children with higher teacher-reported behavior problem scores experienced an increase in child-related stress over time, whereas mothers of children with lower teacher-reported behavior problems experienced a fairly stable and moderate level of stress over time. In contrast, the trajectories of paternal child-related stress do not differ significantly based on teacher-reported behavior problems.

In addition to behavior problems, the child's type of disability predicted child-related stress trajectories for mothers but not for fathers. As shown in Figure 13, mothers of children with Down syndrome experienced a significantly greater rate of increase in child-related stress in comparison to mothers of children in the other two groups. Mothers of children with Down syndrome have significantly lower stress scores than mothers of children with developmental delay during the early childhood period but then have higher scores when the child is age 10 years. In contrast, mothers of children with Down syndrome have stress scores similar to those of mothers

69

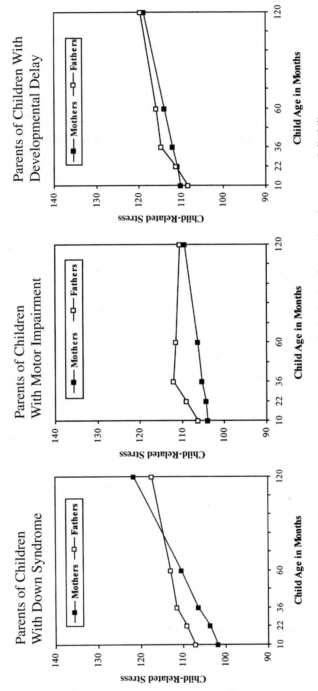

FIGURE 13.— Trajectories of maternal and paternal child-related stress based on type of disability.

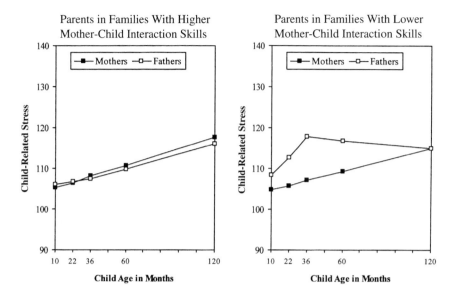

FIGURE 14.—Trajectories of maternal and paternal child-related stress based on mother-child interaction.

of children with motor impairment during the early childhood period. By the time the child is 10 years old, however, the stress for mothers of children with Down syndrome has increased dramatically but the stress level for mothers of children with motor impairment has increased only slightly.

For fathers, in addition to behavior problems, two main effects, child gender and mother-child interaction, were found to be significant predictors of change in child-related stress. Gender was a significant predictor of both the overall rate of change (the slope) and in the decrement to this rate after age 3 years (the discontinuous term). Although the child-related stress level is similar for fathers of both boys and girls when children are 10 years of age, fathers of girls report a steep increase in stress during the early childhood period, whereas fathers of boys report a more gradual increase during both early and middle childhood.

Finally, the trajectories of paternal child-related stress differed for fathers in families with high versus low mother-child interaction skills (see Figure 14). Despite different rates of stress for fathers in these two groups, fathers in families with higher mother-child interaction experienced lower stress scores at all time points until age 10 when both groups reported similar levels of stress.

71

Both child and family measures (but no demographic variables) were significant correlates of maternal parent-related stress when children were 3 years of age (see Table 13). Parent-related stress was higher for mothers of children with more behavior problems (as reported by the mother but not by the child's teacher) and (as with child-related stress) higher mastery motivation skills. Parent-related stress was lower for mothers who reported more problem-focused coping skills and more positive family relations.

For fathers, only lower child behavior problem scores correlated with lower parent-related stress when the child was age 3 (see Table 13). None of the other child or family characteristics variables predicted stress at age 3.

In terms of change in parent-related stress, Figure 4 in chapter III illustrates that there was a significant linear increase in parent-related stress for both mothers and fathers over time. No significant differences were found in either levels or trajectories of maternal and paternal parent-related stress. The analysis of change in both maternal and paternal parent-related stress controlled for the significant influences of negative life events.

Different child and family variables were found to be significant predictors of change in maternal and paternal parent-related stress. For mothers, significant main effects were found for teacher-reported behavior problems and social support and a significant interaction was found between type of disability and mother-child interaction.

As shown in Figure 15, mothers of children with high teacher-reported behavior problem scores experienced a steep increase in parent-related stress over time and mothers of children with low teacher-reported behavior problems experienced a decrease in stress over time. Fathers' stress scores for the two groups increased at somewhat different rates, but the differences in the trajectories were not large enough to be statistically significant.

The significant interaction effect found between type of disability and mother-child interaction indicates that mothers of children with Down syndrome and developmental delay experience greater increases in stress if they have poor interaction skills. Mothers of children in these disability groups who have stronger interaction skills experience a more stable level of stress over time. In contrast, mothers of children with motor impairment do not show different patterns of change based on their interaction skills.

Finally, social support was a significant predictor of change in maternal parent-related stress (see Figure 16). Mothers with low levels of social support reported increases in stress over time; mothers with high levels of

TABLE 13

GROWTH CURVE ANALYSIS: PREDICTING TRAJECTORIES OF CHANGE IN PARENT-RELATED STRESS

	Final Model					
	Maternal			Paternal		
	β_1 (SE) (age 3 status)	β_2 (SE) (rate of change)	$\beta_3{}^a$ (SE) (control)	β_4 (SE) (age 3 status)	β_5 (SE) (rate of change)	$\beta_6{}^b$ (SE) (control)
Intercepts	134.552 (22.70)***	.543 (.26)*	2.856 (1.00)**	137.416 (28.28)***	.454 (.35)	3.570 (1.31)**
Child characteristics						
Type of disability^c						
Down syndrome (DS)	19.431 (27.36)	−.150 (.33)		−2.742 (29.31)	−.203 (.38)	
Motor impairment (MI)	23.889 (23.53)	−.786 (.27)**		19.750 (30.94)	.002 (.37)	
Gender (female)	3.365 (2.86)	.043 (.04)		5.014 (3.16)	−.004 (.05)	
Health	−.007 (.14)	.000 (.00)		.106 (.15)	.000 (.00)	
Parent characteristics						
Years of education	−.041 (0.72)	.010 (.01)		−.037 (.55)	.011 (.01)	
Marital status (married)	6.331 (3.76)	−.087 (.05)		3.494 (4.81)	−.119 (.07)	
Parenting assets						
Problem-focused coping	−28.449 (13.65)*	−.479 (.26)		−23.206 (15.95)	−.526 (.21)*	
Support helpfulness	−.286 (.18)	−.004 (.00)*		−.226 (.17)	−.002 (.00)	
Family climate						
Mother-child interaction (MC)	.893 (.49)	−.007 (.01)		.316 (.60)	−.004 (.01)	
Family relations	−1.971 (.53)**	−.000 (.01)		−.697 (.49)	−.002 (.01)	
Child development skills						
Cognitive skills	.002 (.13)	.001 (.00)		−.054 (.13)	.002 (.00)	
Adaptive skills	−.576 (.33)	.003 (.00)		−.696 (.42)	−.001 (.01)	
Child self-regulatory processes						
Mastery motivation	2.530 (1.13)*	−.027 (.01)		1.688 (1.09)	−.042 (.01)**	
Behavior problems (mother)	5.419 (1.72)**	.019 (.02)		3.802 (1.62)*	−.001 (.03)	
Behavior problems (teacher)	−1.961 (1.00)*	.035 (.01)*		.228 (1.35)	.011 (.01)	
Interaction terms						
DS × MC	−.428 (.71)	.004 (.01)		.255 (.75)	.006 (.01)	
MI × MC	−.559 (.62)	.017 (.01)*		−.445 (.79)	−.000 (.01)	

^aControlling for mother report of negative life events as a time-varying covariate.

^bControlling for father report of negative life events as a time-varying covariate.

^cChildren with developmental delay are the reference group.

*$p < .05$; **$p < .01$; ***$p < .001$.

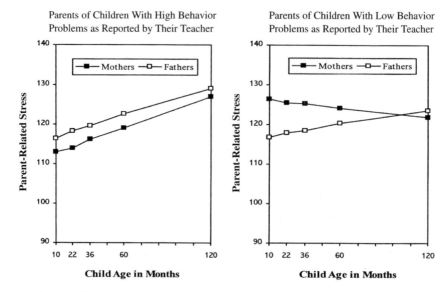

FIGURE 15.—Trajectories of maternal and paternal parent-related stress based on teacher report of child behavior problems.

support reported stress scores that decreased slightly over time. In addition, the stress scores reported by mothers with high levels of support were lower at each time point than those reported by mothers with low levels of support. No differences in the trajectories of parent-related stress were found based on differences in support for fathers.

Two significant main effects of change in parent-related stress were found, however, for fathers. As shown in Figure 17, fathers of children with low mastery motivation skills experienced an increase in stress over time, but fathers of children with high mastery motivation skills reported a stable level of stress. Interestingly, fathers of children with low mastery skills have lower stress scores from entry to early intervention to age 5 years, and then their stress scores increase substantially. When their child is age 10 years, fathers of children with low mastery motivation skills have a parent-related stress score that is about 10 points higher than that for fathers of children with high mastery motivation skills.

Finally, problem-focused coping skills were also a significant predictor of change in paternal parent-related stress (see Figure 18). Fathers with low levels of problem-focused coping skills experienced a significant increase in parent-related stress over time. In contrast, fathers with high problem-focused coping skills reported a stable level of stress over time. In addition, their stress scores were consistently lower than those for fathers with poor problem-focused coping skills.

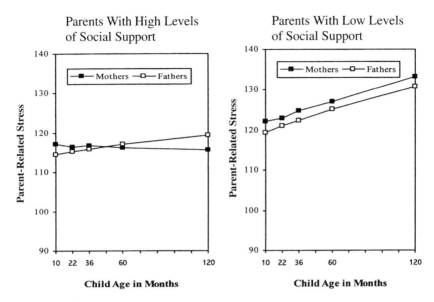

FIGURE 16.—Trajectories of maternal and paternal parent-related stress based on parent social support.

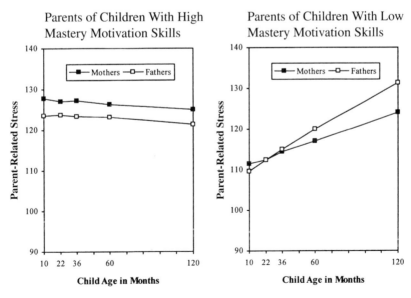

FIGURE 17.—Trajectories of maternal and paternal parent-related stress based on child mastery motivation skills.

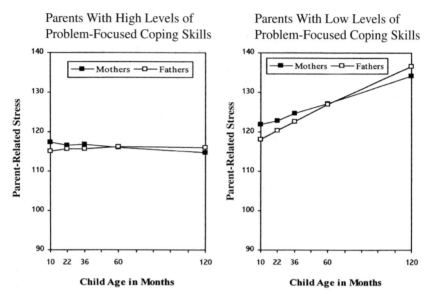

Parents With High Levels of Problem-Focused Coping Skills

Parents With Low Levels of Problem-Focused Coping Skills

FIGURE 18.—Trajectories of maternal and paternal parent-related stress based on parent problem-focused coping skills.

Summary of Findings for Parent Well-Being

Three themes emerge from these analyses. The first theme relates to the similarities and differences in maternal and paternal stress over time. Although the maternal and paternal trajectories of child-related stress were both positive, fathers on average displayed a significantly higher level of child-related stress when their child was 3 years old. In addition, the maternal trajectory of child-related stress was linear, but the paternal trajectory was best modeled with a discontinuous function. For parent-related stress, both the maternal and paternal trajectories were linear and increased more gradually over time than the child-related stress scores. Maternal and paternal parent-related stress scores were similar when the child was 10 years old. Finally, changes in maternal and paternal parent-related stress and maternal child-related stress (but not paternal child-related stress) were associated with negative life events unrelated to the child, such as economic difficulties, changes in family composition, and legal problems. Thus, the analysis of these three outcomes each included negative life events as a time-varying covariate.

Second, only one predictor of change was significant for both mothers and fathers: child behavior problems. Parents of children with higher behavior problem scores experienced both greater increases in child-related stress over time and higher stress scores at each time point than parents of children with lower behavior problem scores. Behavior problems was also a significant main effect predictor of change in maternal, but not paternal, parent-related stress.

Third, other than behavior problems, the predictors of change in child-related and parent-related stress are different for mothers and fathers in terms of both main effects and interaction effects (see Table 14). For mothers, type of disability was a significant main effect predictor of change in child-related stress and a significant interaction effect predictor of change (with mother-child interaction) in parent-related stress. For both of these findings, the changes in stress differed for mothers of children with motor impairment in comparison to mothers of children with Down syndrome or developmental delay.

Different child characteristics predicted change in the two stress measures for fathers. Child gender was a significant predictor of change in paternal child-related stress, and mastery motivation was a significant predictor of change in paternal parent-related stress. In addition, different parent assets and family climate measures were significant predictors of change in the two stress outcomes for mothers and fathers. None of these measures were significant main effect predictors for maternal child-related stress, but mother-child interaction was a significant predictor of paternal child-related stress. Finally, change in maternal parent-related stress was predicted by social support and change in paternal parent-related support was predicted by problem-focused coping skills.

TABLE 14

SUMMARY OF SIGNIFICANT PREDICTORS OF CHANGE IN PARENT WELL-BEING

Outcome	Main Effects[a] (slope)	Interactions[a] (slope)
Child-related stress (mother)	Down syndrome Behavior problems (M) Behavior problems (T)	None
Child-related stress (father)	Child gender[b] Behavior problems (M)[b] Mother-child interaction[c]	None
Parent-related stress (mother)	Motor impairment (MI) Behavior problems (T) Social support (M)	MI × MC
Parent-related stress (father)	Child mastery motivation Problem-focused coping (F)	None

[a]M = mother report, T = teacher report, MI = motor impairment, MC = mother-child interaction, F = father report.
[b]Significant for the slope and the discontinuous term.
[c]Significant for the discontinuous term only.

77

INTEGRATION OF FINDINGS FOR CHILD DEVELOPMENT
AND PARENT WELL-BEING

In summary, children's type of disability predicted different trajectories of development in cognition, social skills, and daily living skills. Children's type of disability also predicted changes in maternal (but not paternal) child-related and parent-related stress. These findings also indicate that, beyond type of disability, child self-regulatory processes (notably behavior problems and mastery motivation) and one aspect of the family climate (notably mother-child interaction) were key predictors of change in both child outcomes and parent well-being. A different aspect of the family climate, family relations, also predicted change in child social skills. Parent assets, measured as social support and problem-focused coping, predicted change in maternal and paternal parent-related stress respectively.

V. DISCUSSION

The children with developmental disabilities who participated in this study are like all other children in two fundamental ways: they are members of families and they make developmental progress over time. The central aim of this investigation was to expand our understanding of how these children and their parents change, and to identify those factors that predict more positive outcomes. In this chapter, we discuss the study findings for both children and parents. In the following chapter, we consider the implications of these findings for policymakers, service providers, and researchers.

One important contribution of this investigation is related directly to the length and breadth of its longitudinal database. Most previous empirical work in this area has been based on cross-sectional designs, and yet the predictors of change in children and families often differ from the predictors of functioning at any given point in time (e.g., Bryk & Raudenbush, 1987). Overton (1998) emphasized that development is about change, and our primary interest in this study has focused on its modeling and prediction.

Previous longitudinal studies of children with disabilities and their families, although few in number and focused primarily on children with Down syndrome (see chapter II), have been useful in charting developmental achievements over time. These investigations, however, have largely been descriptive in nature and directed toward the individual child. Alternatively, longitudinal studies of children with disabilities provide an opportunity to move beyond the simple mapping of discrete skill acquisition in order to address fundamental questions about developmental theory.

Several investigators (e.g., Cicchetti & Beeghly, 1990; Hodapp, 1997; Zigler & Balla, 1982) have applied a developmental approach to studying children with disabilities and have concluded that their emerging competencies follow general constructivist and organismic principles. Recently, many developmentalists have incorporated these theoretical perspectives into a broader systems approach, as exemplified by both ecological (Bronfenbrenner & Morris, 1998) and developmental-contextual models (Lerner, 1996). Despite their growing popularity, however, relatively little empirical work based on these conceptual frameworks has included children with disabilities. Based on the perspective of developmental contextualism, this investigation was constructed to test a number of hypotheses regarding the degree to which important underlying mechanisms that facilitate the development of children without disabilities (e.g., self-initiated activity and interactions with important others, such as parents) are also essential for the development of children with special needs. Thus, the analyses presented here examine whether (and to what extent) developmental change in children with disabilities is predicted by those same mechanisms.

Some theorists have questioned whether the general principles of contextual effects on child development truly apply to children with significant cognitive, social, and physical delays. Kopp (1994), for example, stated that, "in some instances a physical insult such as brain damage could have an adverse impact on self-righting mechanisms despite the goodness of the environment" (p. 13). Sameroff (1995) remarked that the continuum of reproductive casualty "has at one end a group of children who are so physically deviant that they are impervious to the normal range of caregiving experience" (p. 664). The analyses we conducted were designed to address the question of whether children with a range of developmental disabilities are so constrained by their disability that they are resistant to the usual mechanisms believed to affect typical development.

From a policy perspective, another goal of our investigation was to identify the characteristics of those children and families who are at greatest risk, and therefore may be in need of more services than are others, as they leave the early intervention system. To this end, when identified areas of weakness at one point in time do not necessarily predict future difficulties, the constraints of cross-sectional analyses are evident. In contrast, a longitudinal investigation provides an opportunity to map domains of greater and lesser growth, chart individual change in functioning, and analyze predictors of that change over time. As such, longitudinal data facilitate the investigation of both basic questions about developmental theory (i.e., change) and applied questions about how to influence the development of children with disabilities and the adaptation of their families. The discussion that follows focuses on both change and its predictors.

CHILD DEVELOPMENT

The study sample for this investigation was comprised of children with three types of disabilities: Down syndrome, motor impairment, and developmental delay of uncertain etiology. Over the five times of measurement included in this investigation, we found a linear trajectory to be the best descriptor of growth for all three groups, although we detected differences by type of disability in change for two of the three adaptive domains that were investigated: social and daily living skills. Specifically, children with motor impairment had less change in the development of the skills of daily living in comparison to children in the other two groups. This is not surprising given the need for fine motor development in accomplishing such tasks as dressing and feeding.

In the cognitive domain, prior studies of children with Down syndrome indicated that they typically gain about half a month of mental age for each month of chronological age (e.g., Reed et al., 1980). We found a similar rate of development in the EICS sample. When mental age was covaried across time, however, children with Down syndrome had greater change in social skills than children in the other two groups. These findings support those of prior investigations, which indicated that children with Down syndrome display social skills that are higher than expectations based on mental age (Cornwell & Birch, 1969; Morgan, 1979). Dykens, Hodapp, and Evans (1994) suggested that children with Down syndrome have a relative plateau in adaptive development during the middle childhood years, but we found no evidence in support of that suggestion. Children with Down syndrome had linear trajectories in social and other adaptive areas of functioning with relative strength in social skills during middle childhood.

In analyses of other child characteristics, neither gender nor health status were found to be a correlate of either current functioning or change on any of the child outcomes. Carr (1988) reported developmental advantages for girls (over boys) with Down syndrome, but we did not replicate these findings. The measure of health status used in this study was defined initially by the total number of visits to a physician over the first 3 years of life, rather than by a measure of severity of illness or health concerns. At age 10 years, 96% of the children in the sample were rated by their parents to be in good or excellent health. Thus, as a whole, the children in this sample were healthy.

Finally, in terms of parent demographic characteristics, neither parents' education nor mothers' marital status predicted change in any of the child outcomes.

Mastery Motivation

Beyond the potential influence of child and family demographic predictors, we were most interested in understanding the relation between children's self-regulatory behavioral mechanisms and their developmental

81

trajectories. For example, we hypothesized that mastery motivation, defined as persistence on problem-posing tasks, would be an important predictor of differential child change. Our analyses confirmed that it does indeed predict growth in both mental age and the mastery of daily living skills, such as dressing and feeding oneself. This finding is qualified, however, for cognitive skills in children with Down syndrome, which will be discussed below.

Trying to elucidate the mechanism by which mastery motivation relates to developmental change serves to enhance our understanding of the common characteristics shared by children with and without disabilities. During the toddler and preschool years, children become increasingly goal oriented and better able to monitor their own actions in relation to age-appropriate tasks (Bullock & Lutkenhaus, 1988). Concurrently, they develop a greater capacity to evaluate the success or failure of those actions (Stipek, Recchia, & McClintic, 1992). As their goal-oriented persistence grows, young children gain the rewards of both self-correction and successful performance. This leads them to begin to view themselves as agents of action, and to derive pleasure from mastering challenges (Bandura, 1997; Heckhausen, 1981; White, 1959). As they continue to refine their learning processes through experience with both success and failure, children acquire both the social-emotional benefits associated with the feeling of mastery and the cognitive benefits of understanding their errors, thereby promoting their own developmental progress (Bandura, 1997).

This cycle of challenge and success is most often studied in relation to problem-posing tasks designed to achieve specific goals, such as completing a puzzle or learning the cause-effect relations built into a variety of popular toys. Yet many of the typical challenges of everyday life that children must master (e.g., learning to button a sweater, close a zipper, or match a shoe to a foot) also require persistence and self-correction. Therefore, it is not surprising that children with higher levels of mastery motivation demonstrate more advanced competencies in daily living skills.

The finding that mastery motivation was less predictive of cognitive skill development for children with Down syndrome than for youngsters with motor impairment or developmental delay is perplexing. Children with Down syndrome had a restricted range of performance on cognitive assessments at all time points during the study. For example, the standard deviation of cognitive performance scores of children with Down syndrome at age 10 years was one quarter that of the other two groups. Children with Down syndrome were also more homogeneous in the development of their adaptive behaviors, but the differences in homogeneity by type of disability were not as extreme as in the area of cognition.

Children with Down syndrome also differed from other children in the sample in their performance on mastery motivation tasks. When compared to children with motor impairment or developmental delay at age 3 years, they were equally persistent on tasks involving cause and effect (e.g., manipulating levers that open different windows of a box) but less persistent on tasks involving puzzles. The finding that children with Down syndrome were more likely to give up on the puzzles cannot be attributed to fatigue, since the ordering of task presentation was alternated.

Previous investigations have generated a similar pattern of findings about self-regulation related to task completion for children with Down syndrome, but they have not tested their relation to cognitive development over time. Wishart (1993) conducted a series of studies on operant learning and concept development and found that children with Down syndrome were content to accept occasional noncontingent rewards over the more plentiful rewards contingent on their own actions. She also reported that children with Down syndrome displayed high levels of "off-task" behaviors when faced with the challenge of finding hidden objects. Wishart and Duffy (1990) concluded that infants and toddlers with Down syndrome make less efficient use of their cognitive skills in comparison to typically developing children, and that they often "switch out" of tasks, even when the demands are commensurate with their abilities. Vietze, McCarthy, McQuiston, MacTurk, and Yarrow (1983) noted that infants with Down syndrome, in comparison to typically developing infants of the same mental age, displayed similar patterns of exploratory behavior, but significantly less goal orientation. Berry, Gunn, and Andrews (1984) reported that young preschoolers with Down syndrome demonstrated successively poorer patterns of organization in attempting a lock-box problem.

The children with Down syndrome in the EICS sample differed from the other study participants in mastery motivation on only one of the two types of administered tasks. We suspect that the higher levels of motivation displayed on the cause-effect tasks are related to the attention-grabbing features associated with success on those tasks (e.g., a door opens and a figure pops out) in comparison to the more subtle reward associated with the correct placement of a puzzle piece. A fuller understanding of the distinctive learning processes exhibited by children with Down syndrome will require closer examination of those circumstances in which they maintain relatively higher and lower levels of sustained motivation.

Behavior Regulation

The other aspect of self-regulatory processes investigated in this study was behavioral regulation, as measured by both mothers' and teachers' reports of behavior problems. Although mothers' reports of children's behavior problems were correlated with children's mental age at age 3 years, they did not predict change in children's mental age. In contrast, teacher reports of children's behavior problems were not correlated with children's mental age at age 3 but predicted change in children's mental age. Children with higher levels of teacher-reported behavior problems demonstrated less change in mental age. Many of the items on the measure we used for teacher report of behavior problems, the Classroom Problem Checklist (Kohn, 1988), focus on children's disruptive behavior and engagement in classroom tasks and activities. The relation between teachers' reports of behavior problems and change in children's mental age suggests that some children are more engaged in preschool educational activities and therefore may take advantage of the classroom setting in a way that helps them advance cognitively. This relation appears to be equally important for children of all three groups studied.

Family Climate

Finally, we were interested in examining the extent to which aspects of the family climate relate to differential developmental growth in children with disabilities, as they do for children with more normative patterns. The results of our analyses reveal that family processes predict change in three of the four domains of development studied.

Mother-child interaction. Mothers who were more responsive and growth-promoting in their interactive behaviors had children who showed greater growth in mental age, social skills, and communication skills. In terms of social skills and communication skills, this finding was demonstrated for children of all three types of disability, and for those with both high and low levels of mastery motivation. Although a great deal of previous research has underscored this association between responsive mother-child interaction and positive child developmental outcomes (Kelly & Barnard, 2000; Osofsky & Thompson, 2000), the findings reported here represent the first documentation of the long-term developmental advantages of early growth-promoting interactions for children with disabilities.

These findings are somewhat tempered, however, for growth in mental age. Although maternal interactive skills related to positive change in mental age for children with motor impairment or developmental delay, the relation was less evident (although in the same direction) for children with Down syndrome. This finding is puzzling because mothers of children with Down syndrome did not differ in their interactive skills from other mothers in the sample. The findings suggest that the relation between maternal interactive skills and children's cognitive growth is diminished for children with Down syndrome. Nevertheless, this relation remains strong for other outcomes, namely social skills and communication skills of children with Down syndrome.

84

The interactive patterns demonstrated over time by the mothers in our sample paint an interesting picture. In a prior *SRCD Monograph*, we noted lower than expected average mother-child interaction scores (based on the standardization sample) for the EICS sample during the infant and toddler years (Shonkoff et al., 1992). When the children were 3 years old, mean maternal interactional skills were only slightly higher than they had been at the prior time of measurement (T2), and actually fell below the 10th percentile of scores (a score of 39) for the standardization group of mothers with a comparable education level: $M = 37.8$, $SD = 6.0$; $M = 41.9$, $SD = 4.9$ for EICS and the standardization sample, respectively (Barnard et al., 1989). Thus, at the point of their transition from the early intervention system, mothers in the sample demonstrated less contingently responsive interactions with their children than did mothers of typically developing youngsters. This pattern is consistent with that noted in other studies (e.g., Brooks-Gunn & Lewis, 1982; Vietze, Abernathy, Ashe, & Faulstich, 1978), thereby highlighting the interactive challenges faced by mothers of young children with special needs. Moreover, the continued difficulty experienced by the mothers in this sample underscores the fact that their interactive skills do not simply improve with experience, and points to the need for, and potential benefits of, targeted interventions focused on the mother-child relationship.

Family relationships. Beyond the importance of dyadic interactions, other aspects of the family climate appear to have significant relations as well. Indeed, families provide the primary context in which most young children learn about basic emotions and develop core social skills (Harris, 1989). Boyum and Parke (1995), for example, found that the affective exchanges within families relate to both peer sociometric ratings and teacher ratings of classroom behavior. Guided by a theoretical interest in the relation between family systems and social development (e.g., Hartup, 1979), many studies in the child development literature point to the important relation between family dynamics and the social competence of their children.

Only a few investigators have focused on the association between family relationships and child development when the child has a disability. In a study of children with mental retardation, Mink, Nihira, and Meyers (1983) reported that more harmonious family functioning is associated with more positive child socioemotional development. In a prior analysis of the EICS subsample of children with Down syndrome, we found the relational characteristics of families at entry to early intervention to be a predictor of children's adaptive development over the first 5 years of life (Hauser-Cram et al., 1999).

The analyses presented here extend these findings over the entire middle childhood period. Specifically, children in the sample with a range

85

of disabilities whose parents reported higher levels of family relatedness (e.g., a sense of connectedness and expressiveness) when children were 3 years of age displayed greater gains in their social skills through age 10 years. These gains were demonstrated beyond those predicted by mother-child interaction and were not mediated by children's mental age. Consistent with a family systems perspective (Minuchin, 1988), this finding points to the significant role of overall family dynamics and positive models in supporting the social development of children with disabilities.

Summary

The development of children with disabilities is predicted by both child and family factors. Like children who follow typical developmental trajectories, children with disabilities propel their own emerging competencies through self-regulatory behaviors. Moreover, even within the constraints that may be imposed by a biologically based impairment, children's development appears to be enhanced or diminished by the context in which they learn and are nurtured. Together these findings point to the importance of both the child's intrinsic motivation and the effect of positive relationships among family members, especially within the mother-child dyad.

These results offer an important contrast to those that were reported for the infant and toddler phase of this study, in which measures of family processes failed to predict changes in child outcome for the sample as a whole (Shonkoff et al., 1992). We reasoned at that time that this finding was related to the fact that young children generally follow a fairly predictable, relatively "canalized" course in the development of their early psychomotor skills, despite differences in genetic endowment or early life experiences. We further hypothesized that the impact of family processes on the development of children with disabilities would become evident after the children progressed beyond the sensorimotor period and began to demonstrate more complex symbolic and adaptive functioning. The results presented here support that earlier hypothesis. Family processes do indeed relate to children's developmental trajectories, especially in the areas of communication, cognition, and social skills, but these diverging trajectories become most apparent during the middle childhood period. In studies of children without diagnosed disabilities, other investigators have also reported that the relation between children's home environments and their development generally emerge after the sensorimotor period (e.g., Bradley et al., 1989; Sameroff et al., 1987).

PARENT WELL-BEING

We defined higher levels of parent well-being as lower levels of both child-related stress (the parent's satisfaction with the child's self-regulatory and behavioral characteristics) and parent-related stress (the parent's own emotional equilibrium and adjustment to the parental role). We found that these two aspects of stress are predicted by different family features and child skills, and that different patterns exist for mothers and fathers.

Before describing the differential predictors of child-related and parent-related stress, it is important to discuss the overall patterns of change observed in both measures of stress for mothers and fathers, compare the average scores to clinical levels, and assess the degree to which the maternal and paternal trajectories are related to one another. Although child-related stress increased for both mothers and fathers over the entire range of the observation period, the pattern of increase was different. Mothers' child-related stress increased linearly; fathers' trajectories increased at one rate between entry to early intervention and age 3 years and increased at a different, lower rate, from age 3 to age 10 years. A high percentage of both mothers (38.1%) and fathers (43.7%) had scores in the clinical referral range (indicated by a cutoff score that would be expected for 10% of the population) when their children reached age 10. This finding is in direct contrast to the normative stress scores we reported for this sample during the infant and toddler years (Shonkoff et al., 1992). Further, the sharper increase in fathers' child-related stress during the early, in contrast to the middle, childhood period highlights the potential needs of fathers during the years when children are in early intervention services. Fathers have been neglected in discussions of research and services for young children with special needs, and their needs may be quite different from those of mothers (Hauser-Cram & Howell, in press; Lamb & Billings, 1997).

In contrast to the different patterns of change observed for maternal and paternal child-related stress, a significant and linear increase was found in parent-related stress for both mothers and fathers. On average, the parent-related stress scores were a few points lower for fathers compared to mothers from infancy through age 5 years. The greater rate of increase in paternal parent-related stress, however, resulted in nearly equivalent scores for mothers and fathers when their child was 10 years old. Also in contrast to the findings for child-related stress, relatively few mothers (11.4%) and fathers (10.7%) scored above the cutoff level for clinical referral when their children were age 10 (a score that would be expected for 10% of the population).

Finally, a critical finding related to the average trajectories of both outcomes for mothers and fathers is the strong association found between them. Maternal and paternal rates of change in child-related stress were strongly correlated ($r = .65$), and maternal and paternal rates of change in parent-related stress were moderately correlated ($r = .37$). Importantly, the analytic technique we used was able to take account of the dependence between change in maternal and paternal stress scores and identify significant predictors of change over and above that association. No prior study of parents of children with disabilities has accounted for these substantial relations.

Child-Related Stress

The predictors of change in child-related stress are different for mothers and fathers in terms of both the main and interaction effects. These findings can help to identify parents at the point of exit from early intervention who are likely to experience increases in stress over time and who may warrant follow-up services. Relatively few of the children in the sample had excessively high rates of mother-reported behavior problems. Only 2.1% of the children demonstrated evidence of high levels of externalizing difficulties and 3.4% had high levels of internalizing problems, both based on a t-score cutoff at the 98th percentile of the standardization sample (Achenbach & Edelbrock, 1983); no differences were found by type of disability. Nevertheless, higher behavior problem scores predicted greater increases in both maternal and paternal child-related stress. In addition, teacher reports of greater child behavior problems also predicted increases in maternal, but not paternal, child-related stress. These findings are supported by other studies that have also found maternal stress to be at least partially related to children's behavior problems (Hodapp, Dykens, & Masino, 1997; Sloper, Knussen, Turner, & Cunningham, 1991). Further, the fact that maternal child-related stress is predicted by teacher-reported behavior problems, over and above mother-reported behavior problems, eliminates attributing these findings solely to the shared variance between maternal reports of stress and child behavior.

The remaining predictors of change in child-related stress were different for mothers and fathers. Type of disability was a significant predictor of change in maternal child-related stress. When their children were 3 years old, mothers of children with Down syndrome reported stress scores that were significantly lower than those for mothers of children with developmental delay, but their stress scores increased at a significantly higher rate over time. This resulted in an average stress score when the children were 10 years old that was a few points higher than that reported by mothers of children with developmental delay. For mothers of children with Down syndrome, the definitive nature of their child's diagnosis, the availability of diagnostic-specific information and social support services, and the ease with which their child can qualify for therapeutic services during the early childhood period may account for their low initial stress scores. Mothers of children with developmental delay of uncertain etiology, however, have a less certain understanding of their child's delays, less extensive information available, and typically less access to parent support groups. Over time, however, difficulties of obtaining appropriate and needed therapeutic services for all children with disabilities as they enter middle childhood, in addition to worries parents have about approaching adolescence, may account for the increases in stress reported by mothers in both groups.

Although change in maternal child-related stress was predicted solely by child characteristics, change in paternal child-related stress was predicted by child and family climate characteristics. Child gender was a significant predictor of change in paternal child-related stress. Although fathers of girls and boys reported similar stress scores when their child was 10 years old, fathers of girls experienced a steep increase in stress from entry to early intervention to age 3 years, and fathers of boys reported a more gradual increase. In studies of typically developing children, investigators have also reported that fathers often respond differently to their sons and daughters (Nydegger & Mitteness, 1996). For example, DeLuccie and Davis (1990) reported variations in fathers' attitudes of trust and acceptance of their child, based in part on the child's gender.

The final predictor of change in paternal child-related stress was mother-child interaction. Although the rates of stress differed for fathers from families with high versus low mother-child interaction, fathers in families with high mother-child interaction reported consistently lower stress scores at every time point except at age 10 years when both groups reported similar levels of stress. These findings suggest the influence of *mother*-child interaction on changes in *fathers'* stress. Results presented earlier point to the relation between mother-child interaction and increases in child mental age, social skills, and communication skills. It appears that mother-child interaction is also related to paternal well-being, a link no prior study has made. This finding highlights the potential dependence of mother and father factors in the well-being of each partner. Methodologically, it illustrates the importance of using an analytic strategy that incorporates these relations. In terms of policy and practice, it points to the need to view the family as a whole when providing services. Unfortunately, we did not measure father-child interaction, so we cannot test its relation to changes in parent well-being. Future studies will need to assess this potentially important construct.

Parent-Related Stress

Both maternal and paternal parent-related stress increased linearly over time. The predictors of this change, however, were different for mothers versus fathers. For mothers, teacher-reported behavior problems, an interaction between type of disability and mother-child interaction, and support helpfulness were all significant predictors of change. Similar to the results for maternal child-related stress, mothers of children with high teacher-reported behavior problems experienced a significant increase in parent-related stress and mothers of children with low teacher-reported behavior problems reported slightly decreasing stress scores. In contrast to the findings for maternal child-related stress, however, mother-reported behavior problems were not a significant predictor of change in parent-related stress. This suggests that mother's feelings about her own parenting may be influenced by the behavior of her child in settings outside the home.

The interaction between type of disability and mother-child interaction reveals that mothers of children with Down syndrome and developmental delay experience increases in stress if they have poor interaction skills. This provides another example of the influence of mother-child interaction on parent-well-being.

Support helpfulness was the only parent asset variable that predicted change in maternal parent-related stress. Mothers with low levels of support helpfulness experienced a significant increase in stress; mothers reporting high levels of support experienced lower and stable levels of stress over time. These findings match what has been well documented in the literature. Many investigators have found social support to be associated with more positive parental psychological functioning (e.g., Dunst, Trivette, & Cross, 1986), mainly in mothers (e.g., Beckman, 1991; Krauss, 1993).

Finally, two significant predictors of change in paternal parent-related stress were found. Fathers of children with high mastery motivation skills experienced a stable level of stress over time and fathers of children with low mastery motivation skills reported a significant increase in stress over time. These findings likely reflect the fact that children with better mastery skills were also found to have greater increases in mental age and daily living skills. Their developmental success may serve to bolster fathers' feeling of parenting competence.

Change in paternal parent-related stress was also related to fathers' coping skills. Specifically, fathers with greater problem-focused coping skills reported a stable level of parent-related stress over time; fathers with poorer problem-focused coping skills experienced an increase in stress over time. Parent well-being has been found to be consistently better among parents with problem-focused coping styles (i.e., active, planful approaches to stress) in comparison to those with emotion-focused coping styles (i.e., venting of feelings, behavioral withdrawal) (Bradley et al., 1991; Judge, 1998). This finding suggests that services which can support the problem-focused coping styles of fathers may serve to improve their well-being over time.

Summary

The experiences of fathers in parenting a child with developmental disabilities, and their distinctive needs, have seldom been studied (Lamb & Billings, 1997). Increases in paternal child-related stress during the infant and toddler years suggest an important point of intervention for fathers. Further, we found that increases in both types of paternal stress are related to different child characteristics (i.e., child gender, behavior problems, and mastery motivation) as well as the different skills of each parent (i.e., mother-child interaction and father problem-focused coping skills). Thus, key aspects of paternal well-being, controlling for child characteristics, appear to be the nature of the relationship between his partner and their child and the father's own problem-focused coping skills.

Increases in maternal stress were also related to children's characteristics (i.e., type of disability and behavior problems), but in addition were predicted by the relational aspects of their lives as indicated by support helpfulness and mother-child interaction (in combination with type of disability). Given the literature on women's development, it is not surprising that we found that mothers' responses vary based on the relationships within the family (Gilligan, 1982). Surrey (1991) contended that the "self-in-relation" is a central organizing construct in women's development. Women begin to deepen their understanding of themselves as mothers through their relationships with their children, other family members, and friends.

LIMITATIONS OF THIS INVESTIGATION

Like all investigations, this study has conceptual and methodological shortcomings. The interrelations among the multiple systems in which children and families are engaged are far more complex than those represented in our conceptual models. We chose to focus on questions about early predictors of later development to address important theoretical and policy questions, but we recognize that the constructs measured by those predictor variables also change because of, and in relation to, developmental factors. The two subsystems of the family we selected for our conceptual model—the dyadic relationship between the mother and child and general family relationships—are part of a complex network comprised of other important family subsystems (e.g., sibling relationships, extended family relationships). Furthermore, families nurture children within a complex array of external systems that include schools, communities, and other organizations (Bronfenbrenner, 1986). Thus, our models address only a portion of the full complexity of the world in which children and families live.

91

Methodologically, we acknowledge limitations in the way in which several key constructs were assessed. Many of our measures were based on observational data (e.g., mastery motivation, mental age, mother-child interaction), and others were based on parent report. Both types of data are subject to bias. The timing of the data collection can influence observational data, as children or parents may not demonstrate behavior that is typical of their usual functioning at the time the observations are made. Although we attempted to minimize this potential difficulty by repeating home visits whenever the parents indicated that they or their child were experiencing an atypical day, we cannot be assured that all of the study observations reflect truly representative behavior.

Parent report data were collected in different ways (by questionnaire and by interview), but such data are also susceptible to potential bias. Moreover, multiple measures based on parent report have shared variance. Therefore, to the extent possible, we used different sources of information. For example, in measuring behavioral regulation, we used both maternal and teacher reports so that we had data from multiple reporters and settings.

Other measurement issues must also be considered. For example, parent well-being is a broader construct than just the concept of child-related and parent-related stress. Investigations of well-being also might include constructs such as religiosity (Myers, 2000), self-determination (Ryan & Deci, 2000), and work satisfaction (Diener, 2000), among others. Future studies could broaden the focus selected for this investigation.

Finally, because of the limited representation of families living in poverty or families from cultural groups other than European American, the findings of this study can be generalized only to similar families and children. Furthermore, the families in the study sample were all enrolled in an early intervention program prior to their child's third birthday. Although such services are potentially available to all families who have a child with a disability, some may choose not to participate or may be located too far from a program to make participation a reasonable option. Because of the individualized nature of early intervention services and the individualized responses of parents and children, the full effects of program participation may never be known. In a meta-analytic review conducted more than a decade ago, we reported that participation in early intervention services was associated with cognitive gains in the children, and noted that few investigators had studied the relation between services and family outcomes (Shonkoff & Hauser-Cram, 1987). A report on the EICS sample indicated that greater early intervention service intensity was associated with improved family cohesion and increases in maternal social support, but not with changes in maternal parent-related stress (Warfield, Hauser-Cram, Krauss, Shonkoff, & Upshur, 2000). Thus, as Guralnick (1997) maintains, although we do not know the specificity of effects of early intervention, program participation appears to be related to positive outcomes for both children and families. Since all of the families in our study were enrolled in an early intervention program, the findings must be considered within that context.

CONCLUSIONS

In a recent longitudinal study of children with developmental delays, Keogh et al. (2000) reported that a child-driven (rather than a transactional) model best explains family adaptation and children's cognitive and social-emotional competence. They found that features of the child, rather than the accommodations of the family, predicted child outcomes. We reported a similar pattern of results for the infant and toddler phase of this investigation, in which child sensorimotor performance was the strongest predictor of change in both children's skills and parents' well-being (Shonkoff et al., 1992).

In the longitudinal investigation presented here, which extended through the preschool and middle childhood years, our findings suggest a broader spectrum of influences on child development and parent well-being. As they grow older, children with developmental disabilities appear to be agents in their own development, and family processes exert important influences as well. Children also appear to affect the nature and level of the stress experienced by their parents. Although the results for maternal child-related stress are consistent with a "child-driven" model, paternal child-related stress and maternal and paternal parent-related stress are influenced by child characteristics (i.e., behavior problems, mastery motivation, and child gender), the family climate (mother-child interaction), and parent assets (problem-focused coping skills and support helpfulness).

As a whole, the pattern of findings from this investigation indicates support for both the transactional (Sameroff & Fiese, 2000) and developmental-contextual systems (Lerner, 1996) perspectives in understanding the development of children with disabilities and the well-being of their parents. We found bidirectional relations among child and family characteristics, and noted clear influences of child and family processes. Children, to some extent, advance their own development through self-regulatory processes. The relational aspects of the family climate, however, are also important predictors of children's developmental trajectories. Child behavioral regulation and the emergence of specific child skills and competencies, in combination with measures of the family climate and parent assets, are important predictors of parent well-being. In short, the basic principles of normative development also appear to govern the process of change for children with developmental disabilities.

93

VI. IMPLICATIONS FOR RESEARCH, POLICY, AND PRACTICE

From the time of its inception more than 15 years ago, the Early Intervention Collaborative Study (EICS) has been designed to address both a scholarly and a pragmatic agenda. Central to this objective has been a firm belief in the benefits of productive cross-fertilization between those who conduct basic research on human development and those who apply available knowledge to address the needs of vulnerable children and their families. The findings presented here clearly demonstrate the power of such an integrative approach. We conclude with a consideration of the implications of these findings for further study, as well as for the continued refinement of policies and practices.

IMPLICATIONS FOR RESEARCH

Children with biologically based disabilities have been significantly underrepresented in much of the scientific investigation that has advanced our understanding of human development over the past several decades. The findings presented here underscore the importance of that exclusion and demonstrate the clear benefits of not simply documenting children's acquisition of discrete skills but also analyzing the complex underlying processes that explain individual differences in the performance of children with a range of disabilities. Thus, one message of this investigation is that the child development research community can learn a great deal from studying children with developmental impairments and their families. In this sense, the science of child development represents yet another frontier in the continuing campaign to secure full inclusion in the mainstream of society for all children with special needs.

The findings of this study also point to the unparalleled value of long-term longitudinal data for understanding the *process* of developmental change. Thus, although diverging trajectories often begin during the early childhood years, the distinctions among individual pathways are often not apparent in cross-sectional investigations or short-term studies that extend over relatively brief intervals. For example, several discrepancies have been identified between findings reported for the first phase of the EICS (which covered only one year) and those developed from the longitudinal analyses reported here. In analyses conducted at the end of the first phase, we found no significant relation between features of the caregiving environment and change in children's psychomotor and adaptive skills (Shonkoff et al., 1992). We also found that few mothers or fathers (less than 10%) reported experiencing extremely high levels of either child-related or parent-related stress (i.e., above the clinical cutoff criterion), and noted little change in maternal and paternal stress scores over the one-year period.

After following these children and families for a longer period of time, different patterns have emerged. These longitudinal analyses point to the central role of family processes in children's development and in influencing maternal and paternal stress both directly and by moderating the relation between children's self-regulatory processes and maternal and paternal stress. Although longitudinal studies are vulnerable to many methodological problems, such as restricted samples, inadequate measures of changing constructs, and cohort effects, among others (Lerner et al., 1998), it is only through the process of analyzing change over time that we can truly begin to understand the phenomenon of development. And it is primarily through developing a greater understanding of the development of children with disabilities that we can design more effective intervention strategies to enhance their lives and those of their families.

The science of child development is currently poised for significant growth. Anticipated advances will be fueled by increasingly sophisticated methods for assessing behavior, new technologies for examining the structure and function of the developing brain, and powerful analytic techniques for measuring change over extended periods of time. As the knowledge base expands, our ability to assess the underlying dynamics of development, including the causes and consequences of individual differences among children, will increase. This, in turn, will augment our capacity to formulate, test, and refine the theoretical models and conceptual frameworks that will guide both further study and the innovative application of knowledge to practice (Meisels & Shonkoff, 2000; National Research Council and Institute of Medicine, 2000). For each of these agendas, the full inclusion of children with a broad range of disabilities offers tremendous potential benefits.

Central to anticipated growth in the science of child development will be an expanded understanding of the multiple nested contexts within which human development unfolds, beginning with the critical influences of parent-child interactions and intimate family relationships. As that growing knowledge base highlights the varieties of challenges faced by all families who are rearing children within the rapidly changing context of contemporary society, the importance of understanding individual differences in adaptation will be clear. The opportunity to learn more about the distinctive challenges confronting parents of children with disabilities, and the adaptive strategies that they employ, offers a valuable resource that can inform both our general understanding of the adaptation of all families and our ability to provide individualized support to those with unmet needs.

IMPLICATIONS FOR POLICY AND PRACTICE

Consideration of Family Needs Beyond the Early Childhood Period

When viewed from a historical perspective, the care and education of children with special needs in the United States is a relatively recent phenomenon. Until the middle of the 20th century, the conventional response to the diagnosis of a significant developmental disability in a child was institutionalization or home-based custodial care. In 1968, the Handicapped Children's Early Education Assistance Act (Public Law 90-538) authorized funds for the development of demonstration projects that helped launch the fields of early intervention and early childhood special education. In 1975, the passage of the Education for All Handicapped Children Act (Public Law 94-142) established the right to a free and appropriate public education for all school-aged children, regardless of their disability, and mandated the development and implementation of individualized education plans (IEPs) in the least restrictive environment. The enactment of the Education for All Handicapped Children Act Amendments of 1986 (Public Law 99-457), followed by the re-authorization of the Individuals with Disabilities Education Act (IDEA) (Public Law 105-17) in 1997–98, established an entitlement to an individualized family service plan (IFSP) for all children with an established disability or a documented developmental delay, beginning at birth.

A central feature of the overarching philosophy that has guided this evolving national policy has been a clear and firm commitment to the importance of the family in supporting the child's development during the infant and toddler years. Within this context, there is a vital need for valid and reliable longitudinal data on the relation between the family context and the range of developmental outcomes that are seen in children with different types of disabilities who live at home with their families and receive a typical array of services. The long-standing paucity of such data is highly problematic, and the findings presented here can be very helpful to service providers and parents as they work together to enhance children's development.

When families move from early intervention to school-based services, they experience a transition from a family-focused to a child-focused system. The findings from this study indicate that both mothers and fathers report increasing levels of child-related stress as their children with special needs grow into and through the middle childhood period. In view of the relatively high levels of economic well-being and educational attainment that characterize many of the families in our sample, the high rate of child-related stress reported by both mothers (38.1%) and fathers (43.7%) when their children reach age 10 is striking. Moreover, since school services for children with disabilities seldom provide explicit support for parents (McWilliam, Maxwell, & Sloper, 1999), this relative neglect of the needs of parents may have long-term consequences for their children, especially as they enter adolescence.

Fathers, in particular, have typically been overlooked by service systems despite the fact that they are often quite active in their relationships with their children with disabilities (Lamb & Billings, 1997). Although specific service models have been developed to appeal to men, both in terms of content and logistics (Meyer, 1986), far more attention must be paid to both the way fathers become involved (or fail to engage) with services and the benefits they can be expected to gain.

Need to Identify Predictors and Moderators of Change That Are Amenable to Intervention

There is increasing agreement within the policy and service delivery communities that state-of-the-art care for vulnerable children and families must be guided by a well-articulated theory of change. To this end, most programs are designed within the context of a transactional-ecological model of development that assumes a dynamic and reciprocal interaction between biological predisposition and environmental influences (Shonkoff & Marshall, 2000). The task facing those who construct intervention strategies, however, goes beyond the identification of key predictors, mediators, and moderators of desired developmental outcomes. The real challenge is to identify variables that can be changed through specific intervention services.

The data presented in this publication point to the significant relation between family processes and children's development, with the dyadic interaction between mother and child appearing to be particularly important. As described earlier, mother-child interaction is not only related to multiple domains of children's development but it also predicts fathers' child-related stress. Thus, the dyadic interactional patterns that evolve between mothers and children potentially affect a number of outcomes for multiple family members, including fathers.

Given the low average scores obtained on the measure of mother-child interaction that was used in this study, it is reasonable to conclude that early intervention services may need to enhance their support of many mother-child dyads, as well as consider continuing that support beyond infancy. In fact, although most research on mother-child interaction has focused on the infant-toddler period, our findings indicate that interactions during the early preschool years are significant predictors of later developmental outcomes. The bidirectional nature of the mother-child interactive system is valuable to consider in developing interventions. Although many interventions focus on the mothers' skills, children's contributions and mothers interpretations of those contributions are an integral part of the dyadic relationship. Several curricular models exist in which interventions supporting positive interaction between the child with disabilities and a parent are incorporated (e.g., Greenspan & Wieder, 1998; Zeitlin & Williamson, 1994), and further research evaluating those and other family-focused models would provide important information about effectiveness (Harbin, McWilliam, & Gallagher, 2000). The current focus is on providing early intervention services in natural environments, such as child care and preschool programs, and service providers may need to consider creative ways of supporting the mother-child dyad (McWilliam, 2000). For example, appointments could be scheduled at the beginning or end of the day when mothers are dropping their child off or picking him or her up. These times may be the only opportunity for service providers to observe how mothers and their children interact. It is also important to note that the dyadic interaction between fathers and their children may have an impact on child outcomes as well, and deserves to be studied.

The findings of this study also suggest that family relationships in general are related to children's development, as both mothers' and fathers' ratings of such relationships predicted growth in children's social skills over time. These results further underscore the importance of addressing the family as a whole, and the need to ensure that the training of early childhood professionals includes sufficient content focused on family relations.

Beyond those results that have general implications for policy and service delivery, the findings presented here also raise some important questions regarding the specific focus of interventions. Perhaps the most intriguing relates to the role of mastery motivation as a significant predictor of greater growth in children's mental age and daily living skills. On the one hand, there is clear evidence of the positive impact of this complex variable. On the other hand, the extent to which a child's mastery motivation can be changed by an educational or therapeutic intervention has been relatively unstudied (Hauser-Cram & Shonkoff, 1995). Moreover, if motivation is indeed modifiable, then further research is still needed to determine how such change can be accomplished in the most effective and efficient manner.

The data on parent well-being have comparable implications to those related to child outcomes, and they raise parallel questions. Although the EICS sample demonstrated an overall modest rate of child behavior problems during the preschool years, our findings suggest that problematic child behavior (even to a mild degree) can affect parent well-being adversely. In fact, many of the minor behavior problems displayed by children with developmental disabilities may be neither atypical nor related specifically to the child's disability, but they can still be troubling to parents. The relation between child behavior problems and child-related stress experienced by both mothers and fathers points to an important potential programmatic focus and suggests that education policy and practice direct greater attention to the mental health needs of children and their parents (National Research Council and Institute of Medicine, 2000; Report of the Surgeon General's Conference on Children's Mental Health, 2000).

Generally speaking, educational systems are often reluctant to provide the extra services required to address child behavior problems (Etscheidt & Bartlett, 1999; Smith & Puccini, 1995). Thus, in a recent audit of special education in Massachusetts, psychological services were found to be the least frequently implemented among the recommendations included in individual education plans (U. S. Department of Education, 2000). In view of the importance of social skills for successfully navigating adolescence and the transition into adulthood, attention to psychological and behavioral needs in early and middle childhood should be a compelling priority. This is particularly important for children with developmental disabilities, for whom intervention and education services have generally focused disproportionately on the promotion of cognitive and communication skills, to the relative detriment of their emotional and social needs (Knitzer, 2000).

Finally, the findings indicate that different types of parent assets (support helpfulness for mothers and problem-focused coping skills for fathers) predict changes in their well-being over time. Currently, much more is known about how support differentially relates to parental functioning than on how coping skills relate to well-being. For example, not only have studies found that support in general is positively associated with psychological functioning, especially among mothers (e.g., Dunst et al., 1986), but that social support that is imposed (such as through mandatory assignment to a support group) can result in significant deleterious effects on parents, especially for those whose need for support is low (Affleck, Tennen, Rowe, Roscher, & Walker, 1989). This more nuanced understanding of support indicates the need for a more reflective focus on the needs of mothers by early intervention personnel. Our finding that problem-focused coping is an important predictor of paternal well-being not only identifies an area where intervention services can work to be more family and father focused but also highlights a relation that needs to be better understood through future research.

Need for Data to Guide Long-Term Policy Planning and Allocation of Resources

The differential allocation of resources is a central feature of all policy planning efforts. In an equitable system that provides a full complement of health, education, and human services, some individuals receive a disproportionately larger share of those resources because their needs are greater. The ultimate key to equity and fairness is the capacity to measure human needs accurately and to anticipate future demands in a timely fashion.

Children with developmental disabilities and their families comprise a markedly heterogeneous population. Their range of potential service requirements includes a wide variety of child- and family-focused resources. Individual needs may differ based on a multitude of factors, including the type and severity of the child's impairments, the nature of his or her strengths, the assets and vulnerabilities within the family system, and the availability and helpfulness of the family's informal support network, among others. During the early childhood period, services for children with special needs are embedded within a comprehensive and integrated family service plan. After school entry, services become more child focused and less family oriented. When significant family needs become apparent, they are generally addressed (if at all) by agencies or programs outside of the school system, most often within the domains of health and human services. This shift from the integrated model of early intervention to the more fragmented world of health, education, and social services creates a complex challenge for policy and program planning.

The EICS findings provide a useful foundation for addressing this challenge. As a rich, longitudinal database with both child and parent dimensions, the evidence presented in this publication provides some answers to the following critical questions: What can we learn from children with special needs and their parents at the time they leave early intervention programs at age 3 years that will help us project how well they will do over the middle childhood period? What are the predictors of positive outcomes? What are the predictors of continuing difficulties? Who is likely to do well with minimum professional assistance? Which children and parents will require moderate levels of specialized services, and who will require more intensive levels of ongoing intervention and support?

The capacity to anticipate differential needs with some reasonable degree of accuracy has important implications for both individual well-being and the good of society. For children and families at greater risk, the ability to intervene in a proactive, preventive manner increases the likelihood of achieving more positive outcomes over time. Conversely, the capacity to identify those who are not at increased risk provides a useful opportunity to avoid the kind of overtreatment which, at best, is a misuse of limited resources and, at worst, can undermine the natural adaptive capacities of children and families. From a societal perspective, the ability to assess relative risk within a vulnerable population of children and families at their point of transition from an early intervention program to a public school provides a valuable opportunity to anticipate future resource needs and plan accordingly.

CONCLUSIONS

The EICS has amassed a rich collection of longitudinal data that provide a unique opportunity to address interrelated issues of importance to researchers, policymakers, service providers, and parents of children with developmental disabilities. The evidence and findings presented here illustrate the value of combining these very different yet remarkably complementary perspectives. The developmental-contextual systems framework, which guided this investigation, has identified both child self-regulatory processes and family processes as critical components of improved development in children with disabilities and better parent well-being. From the perspective of practice, these findings indicate that services should focus more explicitly on children with poor self-regulation and on families where mother-child interactional skills are poor or family relations and parent assets are weak. From the perspective of developmental theory, these findings indicate that the same processes appear to be central to the development of *all* children.

REFERENCES

Abidin, R. (1983). *Parenting Stress Index manual.* Charlottesville, VA: Pediatric Psychology Press.

Abidin, R. (1995). *Parenting Stress Index: manual* (3rd ed.). Odessa, FL: Psychological Assessment Resources.

Achenbach, T. M., & Edelbrock, C. S. (1983). *Manual for the Child Behavior Checklist and Revised Child Behavior Profile.* Burlington, VT: University Associates in Psychiatry.

Affleck, G., Tennen, H., Rowe, J., Roscher, B., & Walker, L. (1989). Effects of formal support on mothers' adaptation to the hospital-to-home transition of high-risk infants: The benefits and costs of helping. *Child Development, 60,* 488–501.

Aiken, L. S., & West, S. G. (1991). *Multiple regression: Testing and interpreting interactions.* Newbury Park, CA: Sage.

Anastopoulos, A. D., Guevremont, D. C., Shelton, T. L., & DuPaul, G. J. (1992). Parenting stress among families of children with attention deficit hyperactivity disorder. *Journal of Abnormal Child Psychology, 20,* 503–520.

Anderson, K. E., Lytton, H., & Romney, D. M. (1986). Mothers' interaction with normal and conduct-disordered boys: Who affects whom? *Developmental Psychology, 22,* 604–609.

Bandura, A. (1997). *Self-efficacy: The exercise of control.* New York: Freeman.

Barnard, K. E. (1978). *Nursing Child Assessment Teaching Scales.* Seattle: University of Washington School of Nursing.

Barnard, K. E. (1997). Influencing parent-child interactions for children at risk. In M. J. Guralnick (Ed.), *The effectiveness of early intervention.* Baltimore: Brookes.

Barnard, K. E., Hammond, M. A., Booth, C. L., Bee, H. L., Mitchell, S. K., & Spieker, S. J. (1989). Measurement and meaning of parent-child interaction. In F. J. Morrison, C. Lord, & D. P. Keating (Eds.), *Applied developmental psychology Vol. 3.* New York: Academic Press.

Barnard, K. E., & Kelly, J. F. (1990). Assessment of parent-child interaction. In S. J. Meisels & J. P. Shonkoff (Eds.), *Handbook of early childhood intervention.* New York: Cambridge University Press.

Baron, R. M., & Kenny, D. A. (1986). The moderator-mediator variable distinction in social psychological research: Conceptual, strategic, and statistical considerations. *Journal of Personality and Social Psychology, 51,* 1173–1182.

Bayley, N. (1969). *The Scales of Infant Development.* New York: Psychological Corp.

Beckman, P. J. (1991). Comparison of mothers' and fathers' perceptions of the effect of young children with and without disabilities. *American Journal on Mental Retardation, 95,* 585–595.

Beeghly, M., & Cicchetti, D. (1987). An organizational approach to symbolic development in children with Down syndrome. In D. Cicchetti & M. Beeghly (Eds.), *Symbolic development in atypical children.* San Francisco: Jossey-Bass.

Bennett, F. C., Sells, C. J., & Brand, C. (1979). Influences on measured intelligence in children with Down's syndrome. *American Journal of Diseases in Childhood*, **50**, 383–386.

Berry, P., Gunn, P., & Andrews, R. J. (1984). The behaviour of Down's syndrome children using the 'Lock Box': A research note. *Journal of Child Psychology and Psychiatry*, **25**, 125–131.

Binet, A., & Simon, T. (1916). *The development of intelligence in children*. Vineland, NJ: Publications of the Training School at Vineland. (Reprinted by Williams Publishing Co., Nashville, TN, 1980.)

Bornstein, M. H., & Tamis-LeMonda, C. S. (1989). Maternal responsiveness and cognitive development. In M. H. Bornstein (Ed.), *Maternal responsiveness: Characteristics and consequences*. San Francisco: Jossey-Bass.

Boyum, L. A., & Parke, R. D. (1995). The role of family emotional expressiveness in the development of children's social competence. *Journal of Marriage and the Family*, **57**, 593–608.

Bradley, R., Caldwell, B., Rock, S., Barnard, K., Gray, C., Siegel, L., Ramey, C., Gottfried, A., & Johnson, D. (1989). Home environment and cognitive development in the first 3 years of life: A collaborative study involving six sites and three ethnic groups in North America. *Developmental Psychology*, **25**, 217–235.

Bradley, R. H., Rock, S. L., Whiteside, L., Caldwell, B. M., & Brisby, J. (1991). Dimensions of parenting in families having children with disabilities. *Exceptionality*, **2**, 41–61.

Brandtstädter, J. (1998). Action perspectives on human development. In W. Damon (Series Ed.) & R. M. Lerner (Vol. Ed.), *Handbook of child psychology: Vol 1. Theoretical models of human development* (5th ed.). New York: Wiley.

Breen, M. J., & Barkley, R. A. (1988). Child psychopathology and parenting stress in girls and boys having attention deficit disorder with hyperactivity. *Journal of Pediatric Psychology*, **13**, 265–280.

Breslau, N., & Davis, G. C. (1986). Chronic stress and major depression. *Archives of General Psychiatry*, **43**, 309–314.

Bristol, M. M., Gallagher, J. J., & Schopler, E. (1988). Mothers and fathers of young developmentally disabled and nondisabled boys: Adaptation and spousal support. *Developmental Psychology*, **24**, 441–451.

Bronfenbrenner, U. (1979). *The ecology of human development*. Cambridge, MA: Harvard University Press.

Bronfenbrenner, U. (1986). Ecology of the family as a context for human development: Research perspectives. *Developmental Psychology*, **22**, 723–742.

Bronfenbrenner, U., & Morris, P. A. (1998). The ecology of developmental processes. In W. Damon (Series Ed.) & R. M. Lerner (Vol. Ed.), *Handbook of child psychology: Vol. 1. Theoretical models of human development* (5th ed.). New York: Wiley.

Bronson, M. B. (2000). *Self-regulation in early education*. New York: Guilford.

Brooks-Gunn, J., & Lewis, M. (1982). Development of play behavior in handicapped and normal infants. *Topics in Early Childhood Special Education*, **2**, 14–27.

Bruner, J. (1996). *The culture of education*. Cambridge, MA: Harvard University Press.

Bryk, A. S., & Raudenbush, S. W. (1987). Application of hierarchical linear models to assessing change. *Psychological Bulletin*, **101**, 147–158.

Bullock, M., & Lutkenhaus, P. (1988). The development of volitional behavior in the toddler years. *Child Development*, **59**, 664–674.

Burchinal, M. R. (1999). Statistical methods for describing developmental patterns. *Early Education and Development*, **10**, 83–99.

Burchinal, M. R., Bailey, D. B., & Snyder, P. (1994). Using growth curve analysis to evaluate child change in longitudinal investigations. *Journal of Early Intervention*, **18**, 403–423.

Caldwell, B. M. (1973). The importance of beginning early. In M. B. Karnes (Ed.), *Not all little wagons are red: The exceptional child's early years.* Arlington, VA: Council for Exceptional Children.

Carr, J. (1988). Six months to twenty-one years old: A longitudinal study of children with Down's syndrome and their families. *Journal of Child Psychology and Psychiatry, 29,* 407–431.

Carr, J. (1995). *Down's syndrome: Children growing up.* Cambridge, UK: Cambridge University Press.

Cicchetti, D., & Beeghly, M. (1990). *Children with Down syndrome: A developmental perspective.* New York: Cambridge University Press.

Cornwell, A., & Birch, H. G. (1969). Psychological and social development in home-reared children with Down's syndrome (mongolism). *American Journal of Mental Deficiency, 70,* 341–350.

Costigan, C. L., Floyd, F. J., Harter, K. S., & McClintock, J. C. (1997). Family process and adaptation to children with mental retardation: Disruption and resilience in family problem-solving interactions. *Journal of Family Psychology, 11,* 515–529.

Crawley, S., & Spiker, D. (1983). Mother-child interactions involving two-year-olds with Down syndrome: A look at individual differences. *Child Development, 54,* 1312–1323.

Crnic, K., Friedrich, W., & Greenberg, M. (1983). Adaptation of families with mentally retarded children: A model of stress, coping, and family ecology. *American Journal on Mental Retardation, 88,* 125–138.

Dameron, L. (1963). Development of intelligence in infants with mongolism. *Child Development, 34,* 733–738.

DeLuccie, M. F., & Davis, A. J. (1990). Father-child relationships from the preschool years through mid-adolescence. *The Journal of Genetic Psychology, 152,* 225–238.

Dicks-Mireaux, M. J. (1972). Mental development of infants with Down syndrome. *American Journal of Mental Deficiency, 77,* 26–32.

Diener, E. (2000). Subjective well-being: The science of happiness and a proposal for a national index. *American Psychologist, 55,* 34–43.

Doss, L. S., & Reichle, J. (1989). Establishing communicative alternatives to the emissions of socially motivated excess behavior: A review. *Journal of the Association for Persons with Severe Handicaps, 14,* 101–112.

Duis, S., Summers, M., & Summers, C. R. (1997). Parent versus child stress in diverse family types: An ecological approach. *Topics in Early Childhood Special Education, 17,* 53–73.

Duncan, G., Brooks-Gunn, J., & Klebanov, P. K. (1994). Economic deprivation and early childhood development. *Child Development, 65,* 296–318.

Dunst, C., Jenkins, V., & Trivette, C. (1984). The Family Support Scale: Reliability and validity. *Journal of Individual, Family, and Community Wellness, 1,* 45–52.

Dunst, C. J., Trivette, C. M., & Cross, A. (1986). Mediating influences of social support: Personal, family, and child outcomes. *American Journal of Mental Deficiency, 90,* 403–417.

Dunst, C. J., Trivette, C. M., & Jodry, W. (1997). Influences of social support on children with disabilities and their families. In M. Guralnick (Ed.), *The effectiveness of early intervention.* Baltimore: Brookes.

Dykens, E., Hodapp, R., & Evans, D. (1994). Profiles and development of adaptive behavior in children with Down syndrome. *American Journal on Mental Retardation, 98,* 580–587.

Dyson, L. L. (1993). Response to the presence of a child with disabilities: Parental stress and family functioning over time. *American Journal on Mental Retardation, 98,* 207–218.

Dyson, L. L. (1997). Fathers and mothers of school-age children with developmental disabilities: Parental stress, family functioning, and social support. *American Journal on Mental Retardation, 102,* 267–279.

Erickson, M., & Upshur, C. (1989). Caretaking burden and social support: Comparison of mothers of infants with and without disabilities. *American Journal on Mental Retardation*, **94**, 250–258.

Etscheidt, S. K., & Bartlett, L. (1999). The IDEA amendments: A four-step approach for determining supplemental aids and services. *Exceptional Children*, **65**, 163–174.

Featherstone, H. (1980). *A difference in the family: Living with a disabled child*. New York: Penguin Books.

Floyd, F. J., & Saitzyk, A. R. (1992). Social class and parenting children with mild and moderate retardation. *Journal of Pediatric Psychology*, **17**, 607–631.

Floyd, F. J., & Zmich, D. E. (1991). Marriage and the parenting partnership: Perceptions and interactions of parents with mentally retarded and typically developing children. *Child Development*, **62**, 1434–1448.

Folkman, S., & Lazarus, R. J. (1980). An analysis of coping in a middle-aged community sample. *Journal of Health and Social Behavior*, **21**, 219–239.

Ford, D. L., & Lerner, R. M. (1992). *Developmental systems theory: An integrative approach*. Newbury Park, CA: Sage.

Frey, K. S., Greenberg, M. T., & Fewell, R. R. (1989). Stress and coping among parents of handicapped children: A multidimensional approach. *American Journal on Mental Retardation*, **94**, 240–249.

Gallimore, R., Coots, J., Weisner, T., Garnier, H., & Guthrie, D. (1996). Family responses to children with early developmental delays II: Accommodation intensity and activity in early and middle childhood. *American Journal on Mental Retardation*, **101**, 215–232.

Gallimore, R., Keogh, B. K., & Bernheimer, L. P. (1999). The nature and long-term implications of early developmental delays: A summary of evidence from two longitudinal studies. In L. M. Glidden (Ed.), *International review of research in mental retardation (Vol. 22)*. San Diego: Academic Press.

Gesell, A. (1925). *The mental growth of the preschool child*. New York: Macmillan.

Gilligan, C. (1982). *In a different voice*. Cambridge, MA: Harvard University Press.

Glidden, L. M., & Floyd, F. J. (1997). Disaggregating parental depression and family stress in assessing families of children with developmental disabilities: A multisample analysis. *American Journal on Mental Retardation*, **102**, 250–266.

Golden, W., & Pashayan, H. M. (1976). The effect of parental education on the eventual mental development of non-institutionalized children with Down syndrome. *The Journal of Pediatrics*, **89**, 603–605.

Gottman, J. M, Katz, I. F., & Hooven, C. (1996). Parental meta-emotion philosophy and the emotional life of families: Theoretical models and preliminary data. *Journal of Family Psychology*, **10**, 243–268.

Gowen, J. W., Johnson-Martin, N., Goldman, B., & Appelbaum, M. (1989). Feelings of depression and parenting competence of mothers of handicapped and non-handicapped infants: A longitudinal study. *American Journal on Mental Retardation*, **94**, 259–271.

Greenspan, S. I., & Wieder, S. (1998). *The child with special needs: Encouraging intellectual and emotional growth*. Reading, MA: Addison Wesley.

Gunn, P., & Crombie, M. (1996). Language and speech. In B. Stratford & P. Gunn (Eds.), *New approaches to Down syndrome*. London: Cassell.

Gunn, P., & Cuskelly, M. (1991). Down syndrome temperament: The stereotype at middle childhood and adolescence. *International Journal of Disability, Development and Education*, **38**, 59–70.

Guralnick, M. J. (1997). Second-generation research in the field of early intervention. In M. J. Guralnick (Ed.), *The effectiveness of early intervention*. Baltimore: Brookes.

Guralnick, M. J. (in press). A developmental systems model for early intervention. *Infants and Young Children.*

Hanson, M. J., & Hanline, M. F. (1990). Parenting a child with a disability: A longitudinal study of parental stress and adaptation. *Journal of Early Intervention, 14,* 234–248.

Harbin, G. L., McWilliam, R. A., & Gallagher, J. J. (2000). Services for young children with disabilities and their families. In J. P. Shonkoff & S. J. Meisels (Eds.), *Handbook of early childhood intervention* (2nd ed.). New York: Cambridge University Press.

Harris, P. (1989). *Children and emotions: The development of psychological understanding.* New York: Basil Blackwell.

Harris, V. S., & McHale, S. M. (1989). Family life problems, daily caregiving activities, and psychological well-being of mothers of mentally retarded children. *American Journal on Mental Retardation, 94,* 231–239.

Harrison, P. (1987). Research with adaptive behavior scales. *Journal of Special Education, 21,* 37–68.

Harter, S. (1974). Pleasure derived by children from cognitive challenge and mastery. *Child Development, 45,* 661–669.

Harter, S. (1978). Effectance motivation reconsidered: Toward a developmental model. *Human Development, 1,* 34–64.

Harter, S. (1981). A model of mastery motivation in children: Individual differences and developmental change. In W. A. Collins (Ed.), *The Minnesota symposium on child psychology: Vol. 14. Aspects of the development of competence.* Hillsdale, NJ: Erlbaum.

Hartup, W. W. (1979). The social worlds of childhood. *American Psychologist, 34,* 944–950.

Hauser-Cram, P. (1996). Mastery motivation in toddlers with developmental disabilities. *Child Development, 67,* 236–248.

Hauser-Cram, P., & Howell, A. (in press). Disabilities and development. In R. M. Lerner, M. A. Easterbrooks, & J. Mistry (Eds.), *Comprehensive handbook of psychology: Vol. 6. Developmental psychology.* New York: Wiley.

Hauser-Cram, P., & Krauss, M. W. (1991). Measuring change in children and families. *Journal of Early Intervention, 15,* 288–297.

Hauser-Cram, P., & Shonkoff, J. P. (1995). Mastery motivation: Implications for intervention. In R. H. MacTurk & G. A. Morgan (Eds.), *Mastery motivation: Origins, conceptualizations, and applications.* Norwood, NJ: Ablex.

Hauser-Cram, P., Warfield, M. E., Shonkoff, J. P., Krauss, M. W., Upshur, C. C., & Sayer, A. (1999). Family influences on adaptive development in young children with Down syndrome. *Child Development, 70,* 979–989.

Hebbeler, K., Wagner, M., Spiker, D., Scarborough, A., Simeonsson, R., & Collier, M. (2001). *A first look at the characteristics of children and families entering early intervention services.* Menlo Park, CA: SRI International.

Heckhausen, H. (1981). Developmental precursors of success and failure experience. In G. d'Ydewalle & W. Lens (Eds.), *Cognition in human motivation and learning.* Hillsdale, NJ: Erlbaum.

Hodapp, R. M. (1997). Direct and indirect behavioral effects of different genetic disorders of mental retardation. *American Journal on Mental Retardation, 102,* 67–79.

Hodapp, R. M., Dykens, E. M., & Masino, L. L. (1997). Families of children with Prader-Willi syndrome: Stress-support and relations to child characteristics. *Journal of Autism and Developmental Disorders, 27,* 11–24.

Hyche, J., Bakeman, R., & Adamson, L. (1992). Understanding communicative cues of infants with Down syndrome: Effects of mothers' experience and infants' age. *Journal of Applied Developmental Psychology, 13,* 1–16.

Innocenti, M. S., Huh, K., & Boyce, G. (1992). Families of children with disabilities:

Normative data and other considerations on parenting stress. *Topics in Early Childhood Special Education*, **12**, 403–427.

Jacobsen, J. W. (1982). Problem behaviour and psychiatric impairment within a developmentally disabled population: I. Behaviour frequency. *Applied Research in Mental Retardation*, **3**, 121–139.

Jennings, K. D., Yarrow, L. J., & Martin, P. P. (1984). Mastery motivation and cognitive development: A longitudinal study from infancy to $3\frac{1}{2}$ years of age. *International Journal of Behavioral Development*, **7**, 441–461.

Judge, S. L. (1998). Parental coping strategies and strengths in families of young children with disabilities. *Family Relations*, **47**, 263–268.

Kaiser, B., & Rasminsky, J. S. (1999). *Meeting the challenge: Effective strategies for challenging behaviors in early childhood environments.* Washington, D.C.: NAEYC.

Kazak, A. E. (1992). The social context of coping with childhood chronic illness: Family systems and social support. In A. M. La Greca et al. (Eds.), *Stress and coping in child health.* New York: The Guilford Press.

Kelly, J. F., & Barnard, K. E. (2000). Assessment of parent-child interaction: Implications for early intervention. In J. P. Shonkoff & S. J. Meisels (Eds.), *Handbook of early childhood intervention* (2nd ed.). New York: Cambridge University Press.

Keogh, B., Garnier, H. E., Bernheimer, L. P., & Gallimore, R. (2000). Models of child-family interactions for children with developmental delays: Child-driven or transactional? *American Journal on Mental Retardation*, **105**, 32–46.

Knitzer, J. (2000). Early childhood mental health services: A policy and systems developmental perspective. In J. P. Shonkoff & S. J. Meisels (Eds.), *Handbook of early childhood intervention* (2nd ed.). New York: Cambridge University Press.

Kohn, M. (1988). *Kohn Problem Checklist.* New York: Psychological Corp.

Koller, H., Richardson, S. A., Katz, M., & McLaren, J. (1983). Behavior disturbance since childhood among a 5-year birth cohort of all mentally retarded young adults in a city. *American Journal of Mental Deficiency*, **87**, 386–395.

Kopp, C. B. (1992). Emotional distress and control in young children. In N. Eisenberg & R. A. Fabes (Eds.), *Emotion and its regulation in early development.* San Francisco: Jossey Bass.

Kopp, C. B. (1994). Trends and directions in studies of developmental risk. In C. A. Nelson (Ed.), *The Minnesota symposium on child psychology: Vol. 27. Threats to optimal development.* Hillsdale, NJ: Erlbaum.

Krauss, M. W. (1993). Child-related and parenting stress: Similarities and differences between mothers and fathers of children with disabilities. *American Journal on Mental Retardation*, **97**, 393–404.

Krauss, M. W., & Jacobs, F. (1990). Family assessment: Purposes and techniques. In S. J. Meisels & J. P. Shonkoff (Eds.), *Handbook of early childhood intervention.* New York: Cambridge University Press.

Lacharite, C., Boutet, M., & Proulx, R. (1995). Intellectual disability and psychopathology: Developmental perspective. *Canada's Mental Health*, **43**, 2–8.

Lamb, M. E., & Billings, L. A. (1997). Fathers of children with special needs. In M. E. Lamb (Ed.), *The role of the father in child development.* New York: Wiley.

Larsen, A., & Olson, D. H. (1990). Capturing the complexity of family systems: Integrating family theory, family scores, and family analysis. In T. W. Draper & A. C. Marcos (Eds.), *Family variables: Conceptualization, measurement, and use.* Newbury Park, CA: Sage.

Lerner, R. M. (1991). Changing organism-context relations as the basic process of development: A developmental contextual perspective. *Developmental Psychology*, **27**, 27–32.

Lerner, R. M. (1996). Relative plasticity, integration, temporality, and diversity in human development: A developmental contextual perspective about theory, process, and method. *Developmental Psychology, 32*, 781–786.

Lerner, R. M. (1998). Theories of human development: Contemporary perspectives. In W. Damon (Series Ed.) & R. M. Lerner (Vol. Ed.), *Handbook of child psychology: Vol. I. Theoretical models of human development* (5th ed.). New York: Wiley.

Lerner, R. M., Hauser-Cram, P., & Miller, E. (1998). Assumptions and features of longitudinal designs: Implications for early childhood education. In B. Spodek, O. N. Saracho, & A. Pellegrini (Eds.), *Yearbook in early education: Issues in early childhood educational research.* New York: Teachers College Press.

Luthar, S. S., Burack, J. A., Cicchetti, D., & Weisz, J. R. (1997). Preface. In S. S. Luthar, J. A. Burack, D. Cicchetti, & J. R. Weisz (Eds.), *Developmental psychopathology: Perspectives on adjustment, risk and disorder.* Cambridge, U.K.: Cambridge University Press.

MacTurk, R. H., Vietze, P. M., McCarthy, M. E., McQuiston, S., & Yarrow, L. J. (1985). The organization of exploratory behavior in Down syndrome and nondelayed infants. *Child Development, 56*, 573–581.

Magnusson, D., & Stattin, H. (1998). Person-context interaction theories. In W. Damon (Series Ed.) & R. M. Lerner (Vol. Ed.), *Handbook of child psychology: Vol. 1. Theoretical models of human development* (5th ed.). New York: Wiley.

Marfo, K. (1991). The maternal directiveness theme in mother-child interaction research: Implications for early intervention. In K. Marfo (Ed.), *Early intervention in transition: Current perspectives on programs for handicapped children.* New York: Praeger.

Marfo, K., Dedrick, C. F., & Barbour, N. (1998). Mother-child interactions and the development of children with mental retardation. In J. A. Burack, R. M. Hodapp, & E. Zigler (Eds.), *Handbook of mental retardation and development.* Cambridge, UK: Cambridge University Press.

Maurer, H., & Sherrod, K. (1987). Context of directives given to young children with Down syndrome and nonretarded children: Development over two years. *American Journal of Mental Deficiency, 91*, 579–590.

McCarthy, D. (1972). *McCarthy Scales of Children's Abilities.* New York: Psychological Corp.

McCollum, J. A., & Hemmeter, M. L. (1997). Parent-child interactions when children have disabilities. In M. J. Guralnick (Ed.), *The effectiveness of early intervention.* Baltimore: Brookes.

McCubbin, H. I., & Patterson, J. M. (1982). The family stress process: The Double ABCX Model of adjustment and adaptation. In H. I. McCubbin, M. B. Sussman, & J. M. Patterson (Eds.), *Social stress and the family: Advances and developments in family stress theory and research.* New York: Haworth Press.

McCubbin, M. A., & Huang, S. T. (1989). Family strengths in the care of handicapped children: Targets for intervention. *Family Relations, 38*, 436–443.

McKinney, B., & Peterson, R. A. (1987). Predictors of stress in parents of developmentally disabled children. *Journal of Pediatric Psychology, 12*, 133–150.

McWilliam, R. A. (2000). It's only natural to have early intervention in the environments where it's needed. In S. Sandall & M. Ostrosky (Eds.), *Natural environments and inclusion* (Young Exceptional Children Monograph Series No. 2). Denver, CO: Division for Early Childhood of the Council for Exceptional Children.

McWilliam, R. A., Maxwell, K. L., & Sloper, K. M. (1999). Beyond "involvement:" Are elementary schools ready to be family centered? *School Psychology Review, 28*, 378–394.

Meisels, S. J., & Shonkoff, J. P. (2000). Early childhood intervention: A continuing evolution. In J. P. Shonkoff & S. J. Meisels (Eds.), *Handbook of early childhood intervention* (2nd ed.). New York: Cambridge University Press.

Meyer, D. J. (1986). Fathers of children with mental handicaps. In M. E. Lamb (Ed.), *The father's role: Applied perspectives.* New York: Wiley.

Miller, A. C., Gordon, R. M., Daniele, R. J., & Diller, L. (1992). Stress, appraisal, and coping in mothers of disabled and non-disabled children. *Journal of Pediatric Psychology*, **95**, 29–39.

Mink, I. T., Blacher, J., & Nihira, K. (1988). Taxonomy of family life styles: III. Replication with families with severely mentally retarded children. *American Journal on Mental Retardation*, **93** 250–264.

Mink, I. T., Nihira, K., & Meyers, C. E. (1983). Taxonomy of family life styles: I. Homes with TMR children. *American Journal of Mental Deficiency*, **87**, 484–497.

Minuchin, P. P. (1988). Relationships within the family: A systems perspective on development. In R. A. Hinde & J. Stevenson-Hinde (Eds.), *Relationships within families: Mutual influences*. New York: Oxford University Press.

Moos, R. H. (1974). *Family Environment Scale*. Palo Alto, CA: Consulting Psychologists Press.

Morgan, G. A., Busch-Rossnagel, N., Maslin-Cole, C. A., & Harmon, R. J. (1992). *Individualized assessment of mastery motivation: Manual for 15 to 36 month old children*. Unpublished document, Fordham University, Department of Psychology.

Morgan, G. A., Harmon, R. J., & Maslin-Cole, C. A. (1990). Mastery motivation: Definition and measurement. *Early Education and Development*, **1**, 318–339.

Morgan, S. B. (1979). Development and distribution of intellectual and adaptive skills in Down syndrome children: Implications for early intervention. *Mental Retardation*, **17**, 247–249.

Myers, D. G. (2000). The funds, friends, and faith of happy people. *American Psychologist*, **55**, 56–67.

National Research Council and Institute of Medicine. (2000). *From neurons to neighborhoods: The science of early childhood development*. Washington, DC: National Academy Press.

Nihira, K., Mink, I. T., & Meyers, C. E. (1985). Home environment and development of slow-learning adolescents: Reciprocal relations. *Developmental Psychology*, **21**, 784–794.

Nydegger, C. N., & Mitteness, L. S. (1996). Midlife: The prime of fathers. In C. D. Ryff & M. M. Seltzer (Eds.), *The parental experience in midlife*. Chicago: University of Chicago Press.

Orr, R. R., Cameron, S. J., Dobson, L. A., & Day, D. M. (1993). Age-related changes in stress experienced by families with a child who has developmental delays. *Mental Retardation*, **31**, 171–176.

Osofsky, J. D., & Thompson, M. D. (2000). Adaptive and maladaptive parenting: Perspectives on risk and protective factors. In J. P. Shonkoff & S. J. Meisels (Eds.), *Handbook of early childhood intervention* (2nd ed.). New York: Cambridge University Press.

Overton, W. F. (1997). Marching toward the millennium. *Human Development*, **40**, 102–108.

Overton, W. F. (1998). Developmental psychology: Philosophy, concepts, and methodology. In W. Damon (Series Ed.) & R. M. Lerner (Vol. Ed.), *Handbook of child psychology: Vol 1. Theoretical models of human development* (5th ed.). New York: Wiley.

Overton, W. F., & Horowtiz, H. A. (1991). Developmental psychopathology: Integrations and differentiations. In D. Cicchetti & S. L. Toth (Eds.), *Rochester symposium on developmental psychopathology: Vol 3. Models and integrations*. Rochester, NY: University of Rochester Press.

Pettit, G. S., Bates, J. E., & Dodge, K. A. (1993). Family interaction patterns and children's conduct problems at home and school: A longitudinal perspective. *School Psychology Review*, **22**, 403–420.

Piaget, J. (1952). *The origins of intelligence in children*. New York: International Universities Press.

Quittner, A. L., Glueckauf, R. L., & Jackson, D. N. (1990). Chronic parenting stress: Moderating and mediating effects of social support. *Journal of Personality and Social Psychology*, **59**, 1266–1278.

Ramey, S., Krauss, M. W., & Simeonsson, R. J. (1989). Research on families: Current assessment and future opportunities. *American Journal on Mental Retardation*, **94**, ii–vi.

Raudenbush, S. W., Brennan, R. T., & Barnett, R. C. (1995). A multivariate hierarchical model for studying change within married couples. *Journal of Family Psychology*, **9**, 161–174.

Raudenbush, S. W., Bryk, A. S., Cheong, Y. K., & Congdon, R. (2000). *HLM 5: Hierarchical linear and nonlinear modeling*. Lincolnwood, IL: Scientific Software International, Inc.

Reed, R. R., Pueschel, S. M., Schnell, R. R., & Cronk, C. E. (1980). Interrelationships of biological, environmental and competency variables in young children with Down syndrome. *Applied Research in Mental Retardation*, **1**, 161–174.

Report of the Surgeon General's Conference on Children's Mental Health. (2000). www. Surgeongeneral.gov/cmh/childreport.html.

Roach, M. A., Orsmond, G. I., & Barratt, M. (1999). Mothers and fathers of children with Down syndrome: Parental stress and involvement in child care. *American Journal on Mental Retardation*, **104**, 422–436.

Rogosa, D. R., Brand, D., & Zimowski, M. (1982). A growth curve approach to the measurement of change. *Psychological Bulletin*, **90**, 726–748.

Rogosa, D. R., & Willett, J. B. (1985). Understanding correlates of change by modeling individual differences in growth. *Psychometrika*, **50**, 203–228.

Ruskin, E. M., Mundy, P., Kasari, C., & Sigman, M. (1994). Object mastery motivation of children with Down syndrome. *American Journal on Mental Retardation*, **98**, 499–509.

Rutter, M. (2000). Resilience reconsidered: Conceptual considerations, empirical findings, and policy implications. In J. P. Shonkoff & S. J. Meisels (Eds.), *Handbook of early childhood intervention* (2nd ed.). New York: Cambridge University Press.

Ryan, R. M., & Deci, E. L. (2000). Self-determination theory and the facilitation of intrinsic motivation, social development, and well-being. *American Psychology*, **55**, 68–78.

Sameroff, A. J. (1995). General systems theories and developmental psychopathology. In D. Cicchetti & D. J. Cohen (Eds.), *Developmental psychopathology: Vol I. Theory and methods*. New York: Wiley.

Sameroff, A. J., & Chandler, M. J. (1975). Reproductive risk and the continuum of caretaking casuality. In F. D. Horowitz, M. Hetherington, S. Scarr-Salapatek, & G. Siegel (Eds.), *Review of child development research: Vol. 4*. Chicago: University of Chicago Press.

Sameroff, A. J., & Fiese, B. H. (1990). Transactional regulation and early intervention. In S. J. Meisels & J. P. Shonkoff (Eds.), *Handbook of early childhood intervention*. New York: Cambridge University Press.

Sameroff, A. J., & Fiese, B. H. (2000). Transactional regulation: The developmental ecology of early intervention. In J. P. Shonkoff & S. J. Meisels (Eds.), *Handbook of early childhood intervention* (2nd ed.). New York: Cambridge University Press.

Sameroff, A. J., Seifer, R., Barocas, B., Zax, M., & Greenspan, S. (1987). IQ scores of four-year-old children: Social-environmental risk factors. *Pediatrics*, **79**, 343–350.

Schafer, J. L. (1997). *Analysis of incomplete multivariate data*. New York: Chapman and Hall.

Seltzer, M. M., Greenberg, J., Floyd, F. J., Pette, Y., & Hong, J. (2001). Life course impacts of parenting a child with a disability. *American Journal on Mental Retardation*, **106**, 265–286.

Seltzer, M. M., & Heller, T. (1997). Families and caregiving across the life course: Research advances on the influence of context. *Family Relations*, **46**, 321–323.

Sharav, T., Collins, R., & Shlomo, L. (1985). Effect of maternal education on prognosis of development in children with Down syndrome. *Pediatrics*, **76**, 387–391.

Shonkoff, J. P. (2000). Science, policy, and practice: Three cultures in search of a shared mission. *Child Development*, **71**, 181–187.

Shonkoff, J. P., & Hauser-Cram, P. (1987). Early intervention for disabled infants and their families: A quantitative analysis. *Pediatrics*, **80**, 650–658.

Shonkoff, J. P., Hauser-Cram, P., Krauss, M. W., & Upshur, C. C. (1992). Development of infants with disabilities and their families. *Monographs of the Society for Research in Child Development*, **57** (6, Serial No. 230).

Shonkoff, J. P., & Marshall, P. C. (2000). The biology of developmental vulnerability. In J. P. Shonkoff & S. J. Meisels (Eds.), *Handbook of early childhood interventions* (2nd ed.). New York: Cambridge University Press.

Sigman, M., & Ruskin, E. (1999). Continuity and change in the social competence of children with autism, Down syndrome, and developmental delays. *Monographs of the Society for Research in Child Development*, **64** (1, Serial No. 256).

Skinner, B. F. (1953). *Science and human behavior*. New York: Macmillan.

Sloper, P., Knussen, C., Turner, S., & Cunningham, C. (1991). Factors related to stress and satisfaction with life in families of children with Down's syndrome. *Journal of Child Psychology & Psychiatry*, **32**, 655–676.

Smith, T. E. C., & Puccini, I. K. (1995). Position statement: Secondary school curriculum and policy issues for students with mental retardation. *Education and Training in Mental Retardation and Developmental Disabilities*, **30**, 275–282.

Sparrow, S., Balla, D., & Cicchetti, D. (1984). *Vineland Adaptive Behavior Scales: Expanded form manual*. Circle Pines, MN: American Guidance Service.

Sroufe, L. A., & Rutter, M. (1984). The domain of developmental psychopathology. *Child Development*, **54**, 173–189.

Stipek, D. J., Recchia, S., & McClintic, S. M. (1992). Self-evaluation in young children. *Monographs of the Society for Research in Child Development*, **57** (1, Serial No. 226).

Surrey, J. L. (1991). The self-in-relation: A theory of women's development. In J. V. Jordan, A. G. Kaplan, J. B. Miller, I. P. Stiver, & J. L. Surrey (Eds.), *Women's growth in connection*. New York: Guilford Press.

Thalen, E., & Smith, L. B. (1998). Dynamic systems theories. In W. Damon (Series Ed.) & R. M. Lerner (Vol. Ed.), *Handbook of child psychology: Vol 1. Theoretical models of human development*. (5th ed.). New York: Wiley.

Thorndike, R., Hagen, E., & Sattler, J. (1986). *Stanford-Binet Intelligence Scale, fourth edition*. Chicago: The Riverside Publishing Company.

U.S. Bureau of the Census. (1990). *Census of population: Education in the United States* (CP 3-4). Washington, DC: U.S. Government Printing Office.

U.S. Bureau of the Census. (1992). *Survey of income and program participation 1991 panel: Technical documentation* (June 1992 revision). Washington, DC: U.S. Department of Commerce.

U.S. Department of Education. (1996-97). *Common core of data, school, and agency universe*. (NCES 98-204) Washington, DC: National Center for Education Statistics.

U.S. Department of Education. (2000). *Office of Special Education Programs, State of Massachusetts monitoring report*. Washington, DC.: Author.

Vietze, P. M., Abernathy, S. R., Ashe, M. L., & Faulstich, G. (1978). Contingency interactions between mothers and their developmentally delayed infants. In G. P. Sackett (Ed.), *Observing behavior: Theory and applications in mental retardation*. Baltimore: University Park Press.

Vietze, P. M., McCarthy, M., McQuiston, S., MacTurk, R., & Yarrow, L. (1983). Attention and exploratory behavior in infants with Down syndrome. In T. Field & A. Sousted (Eds.), *Infants born at risk: Physiological, perceptual, and cognitive processes*. New York: Grune & Stratton.

Vitaliano, P. P., Maiuro, R. D., Russo, J., & Becker, J. (1987). Raw versus relative scores in the assessment of coping strategies. *Journal of Behavioral Medicine*, **10**, 1–18.

111

Wallander, J. L., Varni, J. W., Babani, L., Banis, H. T., & Wilcox, K. T. (1989). Family resources as resistance factors for psychological maladjustment in chronically ill and handicapped children. *Journal of Pediatric Psychology*, **14**, 157–173.

Warfield, M. E., Hauser-Cram, P., Krauss, M. W., Shonkoff, J. P., & Upshur, C. C. (2000). The effect of early intervention services on maternal well-being. *Early Education and Development*, **11**, 499–517.

Warfield, M. E., Krauss, M. W., Hauser-Cram, P., Upshur, C. C., & Shonkoff, J. P. (1999). Adaptation during early childhood among mothers of children with disabilities. *Journal of Developmental and Behavioral Pediatrics*, **20**, 9–16.

Watson, J. (1928). *Psychological care of infant and child*. New York: Norton.

Werner, E. E. (2000). Protective factors and individual resilience. In J. P. Shonkoff & S. J. Meisels (Eds.), *Handbook of early childhood intervention* (2nd ed.). New York: Cambridge University Press.

Werner, H., & Kaplan, B. (1963). *Symbol formation*. New York: Wiley.

Werner, H., & Strauss, A. (1939). Problems and methods of functional analysis in mentally deficient children. *Journal of Abnormal and Social Psychology*, **34**, 37–62.

White, R. W. (1959). Motivation reconsidered: The concept of competence. *Psychological Review*, **66**, 297–333.

Willet, J. B. (1988). Questions and answers in the measurement of change. In E. Z. Rothkopf (Ed.), *Review of research in education (Vol. 15)*. Washington, DC: American Educational Research Association.

Wishart, J. G. (1993). The development of learning difficulties in children with Down's syndrome. *Journal of Intellectual Disability Research*, **37**, 389–403.

Wishart, J. G., & Duffy, L. (1990). Instability of performance on cognitive tests in infants and young children with Down's syndrome. *British Journal of Educational Psychology*, **60**, 10–22.

Yarrow, L. J., McQuiston, S., MacTurk, R. H., McCarthy, M. E., Klein, R. P., & Vietze, P. M. (1983). Assessment of mastery motivation during the first year of life: Contemporaneous and cross-age relationships. *Developmental Psychology*, **19**, 159–171.

Zeitlin, S., & Williamson, G. G. (1994). *Coping in young children: Early intervention practices to enhance adaptive behavior and resilience*. Baltimore: Brookes.

Zigler, E. (1967). Familial mental retardation: A continuing dilemma. *Science*, **155**, 292–298.

Zigler, E. (1969). Developmental versus difference theories of retardation and the problem of motivation. *American Journal of Mental Deficiency*, **73**, 536–556.

Zigler, E., & Balla, D. (1982). Motivational and personality factors in the performance of the retarded. In E. Zigler & D. Balla (Eds.), *Mental retardation: The developmental-difference controversy*. Hillsdale, NJ: Erlbaum.

ACKNOWLEDGMENTS

The Early Intervention Collaborative Study was supported by grants MCJ-250533, MCJ-250583, and MCJ-250644 from the Maternal and Child Health Bureau (Title V, Social Security Act), Health Resources and Services Administration, U.S. Department of Health and Human Services, and grants from the Massachusetts Department of Education, Bureau of Early Childhood, the Jessie B. Cox Charitable Trust, Boston, the Foundation for Child Development, and the John D. and Catherine T. MacArthur Foundation Research Network on Successful Pathways through Middle Childhood.

We would like to thank the children and families who participated in this project and who gave so generously of their time and spirit. We also thank the teachers and service providers who assisted us in numerous ways, willingly completing forms and questionnaires. Our Parent Advisory Board deserves special mention for their critical guidance throughout this project. They include the following: Frank Galligan, Realer Hamilton, Phyllis Hannon, John M. Hilliard, Maura Kellem, Judith Lecesse, Dotty Robison, Glen Rosenberg, Paul Schecter, Penny Tannenbaum, Jan Tobin, and Linda Wells.

The participants in this project remained enthusiastic largely because of the sensitive and skillful work of our extraordinary Research Coordinator, Ann Steele. She guided many field staff, came to know many of the families over the years, and always contributed more than her share to this project. We also owe much gratitude to the many individuals who were part of the field staff: Kathy Antaki, Seny Baum, Helene Chaika Fausold, Caroline Fish, Joanne Giuttari, Ilda C. King, Elaine LeClair, Norma Lee, Patricia McLean, Mary Muse, Ann Odessey, Deborah Pease, Patricia Place, Martha Pott, Naomi Schiffman, Karen Stiles, Elaine Dyer Tarquinio, Ann Taylor, Michael Thomasgard, Dot Marsden, Kathy Van Schoick, and Peggy Vaughan.

We received outstanding secretarial and graphic assistance from Dottie Cochrane, Veronica Haytayan, and Jean McCoy, and library research assistance from Angela Howell, and we thank them.

We extend a special note of appreciation to Gontran Lamberty and the Research Review Committees from the Maternal and Child Health Bureau, Health Resources and Services Administration, Department of Health and Human Services, and to Woodie Kessel, Vince Hutchins, and Merle McPherson for the unwavering support of the Maternal and Child Health Bureau since the inception of the study. We also thank Alice Barton, Elisabeth Schaefer, and Marcia Mittnacht at the Massachusetts Department of Education and Deborah Klein Walker at the Massachusetts Department of Public Health for their ongoing support and belief in the importance of this work. Finally, we express appreciation to the reviewers of this manuscript, each of whom provided valuable suggestions, and to Willis F. Overton for his careful guidance and stewardship of this publication.

For correspondence, contact Penny Hauser-Cram, Ed.D., Professor, Developmental and Educational Psychology, Lynch School of Education, Boston College, Campion Hall, Chestnut Hill, MA 02467-3813 (Hausercr@bc.edu), 617-552-8664.

COMMENTARY

ADVANCING FINDINGS, THEORIES, AND METHODS
CONCERNING CHILDREN WITH DISABILITIES

Robert M. Hodapp

This *Monograph* goes to places that few (maybe no) disability studies have ever gone before. Quite simply, there is a breadth of approach—particularly relating to the study's scope and its theoretical vision—that is rarely found in studies within the disabilities field. At the same time, the study's limitations, though understandable, also reflect the field's state of the art. Thus, this *Monograph* describes a critical, necessary study, one that provides a glimpse into the promised land of future developmentally oriented studies of children with developmental disabilities.

In order to understand both the advances and remaining gaps highlighted by this study, we need to reflect on the current state of developmental studies of children with disabilities. This commentary, then, focuses on three advances and three limitations inherent in the present study. Through this joint focus on both contributions and limitations, we begin to appreciate how this study might pave the way for future research.

This Study's Three Main Advances
Basic Information About Children With Disabilities and Their Families

To those outside of the disabilities field, it may come as a surprise that we have so few large-scale, long-term longitudinal studies of children with disabilities. After all, several well-known longitudinal studies exist of typically developing children (e.g., Bayley, 1969; Crandall, 1972), and even children with various emotional problems (e.g., children who act out) or psychiatric disorders (children with depression, conduct disorder) have been the subject of a few such studies.

But, as the authors note, almost no large-scale, longitudinal studies exist of children with disabilities. The authors mention Janet Carr's (1988,

1992) 20-year study of children with Down syndrome, and there are a few other, shorter term longitudinal studies on the development of these children (e.g., Cunningham, 1987). Similarly, there are a few longitudinal studies of children with mental retardation in general, either from infancy into school (e.g., Bernheimer, Keogh, & Guthrie, 1997) or over a few years during the school-age period (Silverstein, 1982; Stavrou, 1990).

In addition to being scarce, the cited studies generally are quite limited in their scope of research. Most focus heavily—at times exclusively—on changes in cognition and IQ. Some provide only basic information about the participants' IQ levels or the changing percentages of the sample at specific IQ levels at different ages. Other issues are almost always ignored. For example, which child, parent, or family variables might influence cognitive changes? How might adaptive behavior develop at all, or be affected by child or environmental factors? Such questions receive little attention in the large majority of these studies.

Similar complaints could be lodged against the studies that examine family functioning. Most such studies look at family functioning at one time—they may correlate family functioning with child, parent, or family variables, but usually these relations are examined at a single time-point. Fewer family studies are longitudinal, and virtually none examine— concurrently and longitudinally—the influences of child or parent characteristics on either child or family functioning.

Kudos, then, for the breadth of this study's design, measures, and analyses. With its examination of 183 children, at five time-points over a 10-year span, this study is long term, large scale, and hands on. It examines children, mothers, fathers, and teachers. Its measures of children include—but go beyond—basic intellectual tests, to also tap adaptive, maladaptive, and mastery functioning. Mothers receive assessments of the child's functioning (Achenbach, 1991; Sparrow, Balla, & Cicchetti, 1984), of their own stress levels, coping styles, and support levels, as well as of their behaviors within mother-child interactions. Fathers are included to some extent (for paternal stress as well as coping styles), and teachers are even involved for checks on measures of children's maladaptive behaviors. Complex hierarchical linear modeling (HLM) analyses are then performed, using both child and family measures as outcomes. This is an impressive amount of work, over a long span of time, bearing fruit in the kind of basic information rarely seen in studies of children with disabilities and their families.

Combined Organismic-Contextual Developmental Perspective

What comes to mind when one speaks of a "developmental approach"? Even within developmental psychology proper, many would ascribe to a focus on the child's development, on such issues as sequences or rates of the individual child's development, or possibly the relations of developments from one domain to another (cross-domain relations, modularity, etc.). Others would nominate contextual factors, examining the effects of the environment on children's development, or even on how children's behaviors or relationships with others might affect families or other systems within which the child develops. In short, these two perspectives—on the child alone (organismic) versus on the child within the environment (contextual)—continue to mark two sides of the developmental coin.

Historically, within developmental approaches to children with disabilities the individual-organismic emphasis has predominated. Consider Zigler's (1969) developmental approach to mental retardation, begun in the late 1960s and continuing in modified form to this very day. Especially in its earliest years, Zigler and his colleagues mostly focused their energies on issues of sequences and structures. Thus, examining those children showing no organic cause of their mental retardation (the so-called cultural-familial group), Zigler (1969) predicted that children with mental retardation should progress—in order—through Piagetian and other stages of normative development (the similar sequence hypothesis). Similarly, like groups of typically developing children, children with mental retardation should (as a group) show no particular areas of strength or weakness (the similar structure hypothesis) (Weisz, Yeates, & Zigler, 1982).

Granted, over the years context has been featured more prominently in developmental approaches to disabilities. Even within Zigler's (1969) original formulation, the idea of motivation was present, mainly in the connection of the child's motivation to a prior history of failure experiences (Zigler, 1970). Later work by Zigler and his students has included more explicit, expanded discussions of mothers, fathers, siblings, and families (see Burack, Hodapp, & Zigler, 1998). As the larger field of developmental psychology has increasingly included more contextualist views, then, so too have developmental approaches to children with disabilities. Still, to most workers studying developmental approaches to mental retardation and other disability conditions, development means "child."

From the other side, for almost half a century psychologists have studied the families of children with disabilities. Various views have been advanced. Some (especially earlier) studies employed the idea that mothers "mourn" (as in a death) the birth of their child with mental retardation. Others, relying on advances in family systems theory from the 1950s on, conceptualized the family as a complex, dynamically organized system. Still other, more recent theories have examined how differences in family support or parent problem-solving styles might relate to differences in how particular parents and families cope. Such changes have allowed for more complex views of parent and family stress and coping.

117

But de-emphasized in virtually all such formulations have been the children themselves. A simple, early example makes the point. In Solnit and Stark's (1961) seminal article, they argued that mothers mourn the birth of what they called the "defective child." This mourning, thought to be a response to the violation of parental expectations, could occur in the presence of any such child—indeed, even twins were thought to disrupt parental expectancies in a way that might bring about maternal mourning. Since that time, many studies of families of children with disabilities have included within their research groups children with widely divergent disabilities, from the relatively minor (e.g., cleft palate) to the much more severe (severe or profound mental retardation). But to this day, few child characteristics beyond age, gender, and IQ are even measured in most family disability studies. Just as developmental theorists have mostly de-emphasized the context and environment in which children with disabilities develop, so too have family researchers paid less attention to the child's behaviors when considering influences on mother, father, sibling, and family coping.

How does the current study fare in regard to the organismic-contextualist question? Exceptionally well. As readers of this *Monograph* will attest, this study focuses equally on both children and their families. Children are the correlates of both child and family outcomes; families are the correlates of both child and family outcomes. One finding, table, or graph of child outcomes is followed by an identical finding, table, or graph of family outcomes. This combined focus on both children and their families is explicit, clear, and unrelenting. This *Monograph* is by far the best—probably the only—example of a study in the disability field that fully employs this dual focus.

Such a dual approach helps this study in several ways. Consider the examinations of child-related stress and children's cognition. Although it has generally been known that the child's behavior problems relate to parental stress levels, less well known is how this process continues over time. But as Figure 12 (in chapter IV) shows, mothers of children with high levels of behavior problems experience increasing amounts of child-related stress over the first 10 years of life. Conversely, the quality of mother-child interactions—as well as of the family system overall—is related to the trajectories of children's development. Although the ideas of children affecting parents and parents affecting children may be mundane in the abstract, such relations become interesting when played out in their specifics.

Operationalization of Basic Tenets of Developmental Psychopathology

Like many fields, developmental psychopathology is infected with truisms. Repeatedly one reads statements about the relations between the child and the environment, of the need to examine the underlying processes of development, of the interrelatedness of various systems or subsystems. In most studies, such statements are usually left in this raw, unspecified state. Statements of this sort become almost mantras for researchers, phrases that are repeated—again and again—but that usually only slightly influence future research.

This study transforms mantras into testable hypotheses. Consider the ideas that humans are active agents in their own development and that "development occurs within multiple hierarchical contexts that are reciprocally related" (as stated at the end of chapter II). By demonstrating strong correlations between children's mastery motivation and later gains in mental age (especially for the motor-impaired and developmentally delayed groups—see Figure 6 in chapter IV), the authors have identified one specific way in which children are active in their own development. Similarly, by examining the effects of varying qualities of mother-child interactions on children's development and of various child characteristics (e.g., behavior problems) on changes in parents' child-related stress, the authors have again specified reciprocal interrelations over time. In each case, the authors have gone beyond vague ideas of "interrelations" to specifically determine just who affects whom over time.

Central to such specificity are carefully chosen sets of measures and statistics. Although one could quibble with certain of these measures (see below), this study does tap important aspects of the child's, parents', and family's functioning. Similarly, through the use of HLM techniques, it is possible to examine the effects of both child and family functioning on both child and family functioning. By beginning with a well-developed, explicit view of human development, the authors then chose appropriate measures and statistics to test theoretical notions that, to others, remain untestable mantras.

Overall, then, this study adds much to the literature on children with disabilities. Practitioners and policymakers will be aided greatly through the basic information it provides concerning both children and their families. Researchers can benefit both from the study's "dual" theoretical approach and its sophisticated use of HLM to answer pertinent questions of child and family influences—on child and family outcomes—over time. This *Monograph* constitutes an important contribution.

Limitations and Questions for Future Research

Given these major advances, this *Monograph*'s limitations seem relatively minor. But just as this study's strengths highlight the field's critical issues, so too do its limitations inform us about the state of the art in

119

developmental disabilities. Keeping the overall, positive evaluation of this study in mind, then, let's explore three limitations of this monograph.

The Role of Etiology

This study begins, but does not go far enough, in emphasizing the importance of the child's etiology on child—and, at times, family—functioning. On the plus side, the authors have specifically separated out their Down syndrome group from others with unspecified developmental delay. They correctly note that many studies, including a few longitudinal studies, have been performed on these children, and that, demographically, children with Down syndrome constitute a sizeable percentage of children in early intervention. Having examined this group separately, the authors then find that children with Down syndrome differ in their trajectories of development (of Vineland Socialization skills), in their (looser) connections between their levels of mastery motivation and changes in mental age, and in their trajectories of maternal child-related stress (a greater rate of increase than the other two groups over this 10-year period).

Thus, children with Down syndrome are different. They are different from other children with disabilities, and even from other children with developmental delays. Although the authors proceed as if the Down syndrome group is different and then do, in fact, find differences, they never quite make this conclusion explicit.

Why belabor the point that children with Down syndrome are different? Because of the particular way in which, over many decades, the Down syndrome group has been used in psychological studies. To this day, many more behavioral research studies examine children with Down syndrome than any genetic mental retardation disorder; computer searches find more than 1,000 such behavioral studies on children with Down syndrome during the 1990s alone (Dykens & Hodapp, 2001). But many of the researchers have not been interested in children or families of children with Down syndrome per se, but instead in Down syndrome as a control or contrast group. We thus see the use of children with Down syndrome as the control or contrast group in studies examining children with autism, with Williams syndrome, and with other disorders. The message (sometimes explicitly stated, sometimes not) is that children with Down syndrome are comparable in their behavior to all children with mental retardation.

As recent studies show, however, children with Down syndrome should not be used as a stand-in for all children with mental retardation. Unlike most children with mental retardation (and even compared to these children's own overall mental age levels), children with Down syndrome show relative weaknesses in grammar (Fowler, 1990), in expressive language

(Miller, 1999), and in articulation (Kumin, 1994). Children with Down syndrome also generally show lower levels of behavior problems (although not in this study) compared with other groups with mental retardation (Dykens & Kasari, 1997; Meyers & Pueschel, 1991). Their mothers and fathers may also experience less stress (though this study suggests only during the early years), and these children often appear to others as extremely sociable and upbeat (Hodapp, 1997). Even into the school-age years (and compared to other children with mental retardation), these children more often gaze toward adults in adult-child interactions, and more often demonstrate social "checking-out" behaviors to avoid working hard at difficult problems (Kasari & Freeman, 2001). In short, children with Down syndrome are different.

A related limitation includes this study's lack of attention to other etiological groups. Granted, such groups are less prevalent than are children with Down syndrome. Still, many of these groups also show interesting—at times unique—developmental profiles, trajectories, and family functioning (see Dykens, Hodapp, & Finucane, 2000, for reviews). Consider, for example, the case of fragile X syndrome, the second most common known genetic mental retardation disorder (after Down syndrome). Recent evidence suggests particular areas of cognitive strength and weakness in these children (i.e., simultaneous over sequential processing), certain areas of maladaptive behavior-psychopathology (ADHD, maybe autism or autistic-like behaviors), and certain trajectories of intellectual development (slowing rates, but only beginning later during the childhood years; Dykens et al., 2000).

And finally, just who are the children in this "developmentally delayed" group? The authors note that these children had "no established diagnosis or etiology that implied a specific diagnosis at the time of entry into early intervention services" (chapter III). The average age for entry into early intervention services was 10 months overall, but just over 16 months for the children in the group with developmental disabilities. This group thus includes any child who was not already diagnosed by age 16 months (on average). Most likely, then, this developmentally delayed group includes some children with autism and others with genetic disorders not necessarily identified at very early ages (fragile X syndrome, Prader-Willi syndrome). Given that over the past decade increasing numbers of studies have been produced on how children with each diagnosis develop, the reader wants to know "what happened to kids (and families) with this or that problem-syndrome?" Even if the diagnosis occurred at later ages, it would be helpful to know the cause of these children's problems, whether children with different (genetic or psychiatric) diagnoses developed differently, and whether their families reacted differently or had different correlates to their reactions.

Need to Reconceptualize Findings Within Earlier, More Specific Findings

The problem of etiology brings up a more general issue concerning the scope of this study. This study is incredibly large in its scope: It measures 183 children, mothers, fathers, and teachers, with a large variety of questionnaires, tests, and interactions, at five separate points over a 10-year span. Its breadth, therefore, is stunning.

Unfortunately, breadth and depth often work against one another. In this study too, depth has been sacrificed, mainly in measurement. As noted at the end of chapter V, the authors well know that both parent-report and observational measures are subject to biases.

The bigger problem for some measures, however, may not be bias per se but a lack of sensitivity. Consider this study's measures of mother-child interactions involving a teaching interaction just beyond the child's ability level. The interaction is coded using Barnard's Nursing Child Assessment Teaching Scale, a 50-item checklist divided into four domains (sensitivity to cues, response to distress, social-emotional growth fostering, cognitive growth fostering). Relying on this instrument as their measure of maternal interactive behaviors, the authors conclude that "The findings suggest that the relation between maternal interactive skills and children's cognitive growth is diminished for children with Down syndrome" (chapter V).

But is this conclusion warranted? Consider other, more specific findings. On two occasions, 13 months apart, Harris, Kasari, and Sigman (1996) examined mother-child interactions of children ages 13- to 48-months old (mean age = 23 months) with Down syndrome. They found that maternal speech that followed the child's lead—that related to the child's focus of attention—was, in fact, correlated with children's receptive language development over this 13-month span. Granted, Harris et al. studied younger children and followed them for only slightly over 1 year. Nevertheless, the question lingers: Are the current *Monograph*'s findings actually due to a lack of association between maternal interactive behaviors and these children's development, or to this study's use of a less sophisticated, more global measure of interaction?

In a larger sense, one needs to dovetail this study's broad, more global findings with other, more specific findings that already exist in the literature. At times, this task will be easy, as this study "extends the curve" over longer time-frames. At other times, one must look more closely at this or that measure, thinking hard as to whether this study contradicts prior studies or instead does not have a strong enough measure of the particular construct. In even such first-rate studies as this one, one encounters the problem of depth versus breadth.

Need to Broaden the Meaning of "Environment"

Conversely, just as certain areas need to be made more specific, others may need to be broadened. To take the most extreme example, this study rightly prides itself on its combined transactional and developmental-contextual framework. As noted above, it is probably the sole study in the disability field to equally address child and environmental concerns over such a long time-frame. The problem, though, is that this project—and the focus of this particular *Monograph*—is on the 3- to 10-year-old period. This time span is the period of formal schooling.

Where are schools in this study? Although chapter VI makes policy recommendations concerning schools, in the study itself schools constitute the predominant environment that is missing. This missing environment would seem more important than communities and other organizations, arguably more important than siblings or extended families (all mentioned near the end of chapter V). In looking at Table 1 (in chapter III), the reader cannot determine how many children in each group attend fully integrated classrooms, how many are mostly in integrated classrooms with part-time resource room placement, or how many children are in other educational options (special classrooms, special schools). Were it not for the teacher evaluations of children's behavior problems, schools would receive no mention at all in the chapters of this *Monograph* dealing with the study itself.

Obviously, it is impossible to examine every environment, for all 183 children, five times over a 10-year span. Something has to give; one cannot do everything. In addition to such practical concerns, there is also the problem of political correctness within the special education field, of the sensitive nature of schools and their effects. Bluntly stated, the effect of different educational placements probably constitutes the most contentious issue in all research on children with disabilities. Various special educators battle over whether all or only some children with disabilities should be included in classrooms with age-mates who are developing typically. Similarly, they argue over the proper role of special education and its relationship to the larger regular education system, and what role (if any) specialized services, special classes, or even special schools should play in the education of children with disabilities. For at least the past two decades (probably longer), each of these questions has torn apart the special education community.

Yet, especially given this study's long-term, longitudinal, and "nested environmental" theoretical perspective, more attention to children's schools and their effects might have helped. Moreover, many of the child measures examined in this study—IQ; mastery motivation; communication, daily living, and socialization skills on the Vineland; maladaptive behaviors—seem heavily influenced by the nature and quality of the child's individualized educational program. For many children, some of these behavioral domains were undoubtedly the focus of explicit school interventions. At the very least, each area of child behavior plays itself out in the school context. Similarly, many readers would like to know the nature and course of parent-teacher relations in groups with disabilities, and the effects of such relations on the child's school success and vice versa (as before, no good disability studies yet exist on these issues). This study, then, has missed an important opportunity to incorporate schools into the list of environments of school-aged children with disabilities.

Approaching the Promised Land?

In reading this litany of three advances and three limitations, the reader might rightfully ask whether the glass is half full or half empty. To me, however, this study—and its role in developmental research on children with disabilities—is best considered through the use of a different metaphor. The study must be thought of as having moved the field along tremendously, but as not quite having reached the promised land.

This biblical metaphor of reaching the promised land highlights both successes and losses. In an important sense, Moses succeeded. His 40 years of leading his people through the desert put him at the precipice, directly looking down over Canaan. And yet, in another sense he failed, never having quite reached the promised land in his own lifetime.

This study, too, has the quality of being absolutely necessary, but not quite sufficient. In the way it provides critical, basic information about the first 10 years of child and family development, this study is unprecedented in the developmental disabilities field. In its consistent use of a combined child and environment focus, it is unparalleled within disabilities and rare even among studies of typically developing children. In its choice of measures and use of sophisticated statistical techniques, it is excellent.

At the same time, however, the study highlights places where those interested in children with developmental disabilities need to go. We need more attention to etiology, we need to dovetail more general with more specific findings, and we need to consider the interplay of child and environment not only over time, but also within the nested environments common to all children.

Let me conclude, then, by congratulating the authors on contributing an excellent, well-done *Monograph*. They have taken us a long way toward that mythical, maybe unattainable promised land—it is now up to us (and them) to continue the journey.

References

Achenbach, T. (1991). *Manual for the Child Behavior Checklist—4-18 and 1991 profile.* Burlington: University of Vermont, Department of Psychiatry.

Bayley, N. (1969). Behavioral correlates of mental growth: Birth to thirty-six years. *American Psychologist, 23,* 1–17.

Bernheimer, L. C., Keogh, B., & Guthrie, D. (1997). Stability and change over time in cognitive level of children with delays. *American Journal on Mental Retardation, 101,* 365–373.

Burack, J. A., Hodapp, R. M., & Zigler, E. (Eds.). (1998). *Handbook of mental retardation and development.* Cambridge: Cambridge University Press.

Carr, J. (1988). Six months to twenty-one years: A longitudinal study of children with Down's syndrome and their families. *Journal of Child Psychology and Psychiatry, 29,* 407–431.

Carr, J. (1992). Longitudinal research in Down's syndrome. *International Review of Research in Mental Retardation, 18,* 197–223.

Crandall, V. C. (1972). The Fels Study: Some contributions to personality development and achievement in childhood and adulthood. *Seminars in Psychiatry, 4,* 383–397.

Cunningham, C. C. (1987). Early intervention in Down's syndrome. In G. Hoskins & G. Murphy (Eds.), *Prevention of mental handicap: A world view.* London: Royal Society of Medicine Services.

Dykens, E. M., & Hodapp, R. M. (2001). Research in mental retardation: Toward an etiologic approach. *Journal of Child Psychology and Psychiatry, 42,* 49–71.

Dykens, E. M., Hodapp, R. M., & Finucane, B. (2000). *Genetics and mental retardation syndromes: A new look at behavior and interventions.* Baltimore: Paul H. Brookes.

Dykens, E. M., & Kasari, C. (1997). Maladaptive behavior in children with Prader-Willi syndrome, Down syndrome, and non-specific mental retardation. *American Journal on Mental Retardation, 102,* 228–237.

Fowler, A. (1990). Language abilities in children with Down syndrome: Evidence for a specific syntactic delay. In D. Cicchetti & M. Beeghly (Eds.), *Children with Down syndrome: A developmental perspective.* Cambridge: Cambridge University Press.

Harris, S., Kasari, C., & Sigman, M. (1996). Shared attention and language gains in children with Down syndrome. *American Journal on Mental Retardation, 100,* 608–619.

Hodapp, R. M. (1997). Direct and indirect behavioral effects of different genetic disorders of mental retardation. *American Journal on Mental Retardation, 102,* 67–79.

Kasari, C., & Freeman, S. F. N. (2001). Task-related social behavior in children with Down syndrome. *American Journal on Mental Retardation, 106,* 253–264.

Kumin, L. (1994). Intelligibility of speech in children with Down syndrome in natural settings: Parents' perspective. *Perceptual and Motor Skills, 78,* 307–313.

Meyers, B. A., & Pueschel, S. M. (1991). Psychiatric disorders in persons with Down syndrome. *Journal of Nervous and Mental Disease, 179,* 609–613.

Miller, J. (1999). Profiles of language development in children with Down syndrome. In J. F. Miller, M. Leddy, & L. A. Leavitt (Eds.), *Improving the communication of people with Down syndrome.* Baltimore, MD: Paul H. Brookes.

Silverstein, A. B. (1982). A note on the constancy of IQ. *American Journal of Mental Deficiency, 87,* 227–229.

Solnit, A., & Stark, M. (1961). Mourning and the birth of a defective child. *Psychoanalytic Study of the Child, 16,* 523–537.

Sparrow, S. S., Balla, D., & Cicchetti, D. (1984). *Vineland adaptive behavior scales—Interview edition.* Circle Pines, MN: American Guidance Service.

Stavrou, E. (1990). The long-term stability of WISC-R scores in mildly retarded and learning disabled children. *Psychology in the Schools, 27,* 101–110.

Weisz, J. R., Yeates, O. W., & Zigler, E. (1982). Piagetian evidence and the developmental-difference controversy. In E. Zigler & D. Balla (Eds.), *Mental retardation: The developmental-difference controversy*. Hillsdale, NJ: Erlbaum.

Zigler, E. (1969). Developmental versus difference theories of retardation and the problem of motivation. *American Journal of Mental Deficiency*, **73**, 536–556.

Zigler, E. (1970). The retarded child as a whole person. In H. E. Adams & W. K. Boardman (Eds.), *Advances in experimental clinical psychology*. Oxford: Pergamon Press.

AUTHORS AND CONTRIBUTORS

Penny Hauser-Cram (Ed.D., 1983, Harvard Graduate School of Education) is professor of developmental and educational psychology at the Lynch School of Education, Boston College. Her research focuses on longitudinal studies of children and families and on change in children's developmental processes. She is an associate member of the MacArthur Network on Successful Pathways through Middle Childhood. She was a teacher of young children and is the author (with D. E. Pierson, D. K. Walker, and T. Tivnan) of *Early Education in the Public Schools* (1991; Jassey-Bass) and numerous publications on the development of children with developmental disabilities.

Marji Erickson Warfield (Ph.D., 1991, Brandeis University) is assistant professor of pediatrics at the University of Massachusetts Medical School. Her work has focused on evaluating early intervention and other educational and support programs for young children and their families, investigating the development of children with disabilities and the adaptation of their families, and examining the impact of parenting a child with disabilities on balancing work and family roles. Her publications include "Employment, parenting, and well-being among mothers of children with disabilities," *Mental Retardation* (2001), as well as several articles on the cost-effectiveness of early intervention services and the well-being of parents raising a child with a disability. She is the principal investigator of an NICHD-funded study entitled "Two-earner families of children with disabilities."

Jack P. Shonkoff (M.D., 1972, New York University School of Medicine) is dean of the Heller School for Social Policy and Management and Samuel F. and Rose B. Gingold Professor of Human Development and Social Policy at Brandeis University. His work focuses on early childhood health and development, and the interactions among research, policy, and practice. He has served as chair of the Board on Children,

127

Youth and Families and the Committee on Integrating the Science of Early Childhood Development at the National Academy of Sciences and the Institute of Medicine. He is a member of the MacArthur Foundation Research Network on Early Experience and Brain Development, co-editor (with Deborah Phillips) of *From Neurons to Neighborhoods: The Science of Early Childhood Development* (2000; National Academy Press) and co-editor (with Samuel Meisels) of the second edition of the *Handbook of Early Childhood Intervention* (2000; Cambridge University Press).

Marty Wyngaarden Krauss (Ph.D., 1981, Brandeis University) is John Stein Professor of Disability Research and the associate dean for faculty at the Heller School for Social Policy and Management at Brandeis University. She is also the Director of the Starr Center for Mental Retardation at the Heller School. Her research focuses on family caregiving for persons with developmental disabilities over the lifespan and on health policy issues affecting children with special health care needs. She served as Chairperson of the Massachusetts Governor's Commission on Mental Retardation for 6 years. She has authored numerous publications on the well-being of families of persons with mental retardation and other disabilities.

Aline Sayer (Ed.D., 1992, Harvard Graduate School of Education) is senior research scientist at the Murray Research Center, Radcliffe Institute for Advanced Studies, Harvard University. She is a developmental psychologist with interests in statistical modeling of individual growth. Her methodological interests include the incorporation of measurement models into hierarchical linear models and latent growth curve models. Her substantive interests include examining the predictors of adolescent alcohol expectancies and the influences of preschool quality on child outcomes. She is co-editor (with Linda Collins) of *New Methods for the Analysis of Change* (2001; American Psychological Association).

Carole Christofk Upshur (Ed.D., 1975, Harvard Graduate School of Education) is professor of public policy at the University of Massachusetts, Boston, and director of the public policy Ph.D. program. Her work focuses on the planning and evaluation of services for vulnerable children and families and encompasses policy analysis and evaluation research on a range of issues affecting communities at risk. Among her publications are *The Government-Nonprofit Relationship: Towards a Partnership Model for HIV/AIDS Prevention in the Latino Community* (Letona, Mills & Upshur, 2001; Elsevier Science Press) and *Significant Health Issues among Massachusetts Racial and Ethnic Minorities: A Policy Paper Prepared for the Division of Medical Assistance* (Upshur, Cortes, Chan, Turner, Besozzi & Mas, 1998).

Robert M. Hodapp (Ph.D., 1983, Boston University) is professor in the Psychological Studies in Education Division of UCLA's Graduate School of Education and Information Studies. His research focuses on the effects of Down syndrome and other mental retardation syndromes on children's behavior, as well as on how such syndrome-related behaviors indirectly affect mothers, families, and others in the child's environment. He is the author of *Development and Disabilities* (1998; Cambridge University Press); co-author (with Elisabeth Dykens & Brenda Finucane) of *Genetic Mental Retardation Syndromes: A New Look at Behavior and Interventions* (2000; Paul H. Brookes Publishers); and co-editor (with Jacob A. Burack & Edward Zigler) of the *Handbook of Mental Retardation and Development* (1998) and *Issues in the Developmental Approach to Mental Retardation* (1990; both Cambridge University Press).

STATEMENT OF EDITORIAL POLICY

The *Monographs* series is devoted to publishing developmental research that generates authoritative new findings and uses these to foster fresh, better integrated, or more coherent perspectives on major developmental issues, problems, and controversies. The significance of the work in extending developmental theory and contributing definitive empirical information in support of a major conceptual advance is the most critical editorial consideration. Along with advancing knowledge on specialized topics, the series aims to enhance cross-fertilization among developmental disciplines and developmental subfields. Therefore, clarity of the links between the specific issues under study and questions relating to general developmental processes is important. These links, as well as the manuscript as a whole, must be as clear to the general reader as to the specialist. The selection of manuscripts for editorial consideration, and the shaping of manuscripts through reviews-and-revisions, are processes dedicated to actualizing these ideals as closely as possible.

Typically *Monographs* entail programmatic large-scale investigations; sets of programmatic interlocking studies; or—in some cases—smaller studies with highly definitive and theoretically significant empirical findings. Multi-authored sets of studies that center on the same underlying question can also be appropriate; a critical requirement here is that all studies address common issues, and that the contribution arising from the set as a whole be unique, substantial, and well integrated. The needs of integration preclude having individual chapters identified by individual authors. In general, irrespective of how it may be framed, any work that is judged to significantly extend developmental thinking will be taken under editorial consideration.

To be considered, submissions should meet the editorial goals of *Monographs* and should be no briefer than a minimum of 80 pages (including references and tables); the upper limit of 150–175 pages is more flexible (please submit four copies). Because a *Monograph* is inevitably lengthy and usually substantively complex, it is particularly important that the text be well organized and written in clear, precise, and literate English. Note, however, that authors from non-English-speaking countries should not be put off by this stricture. In accordance with the general aims of SRCD, this series is actively interested in promoting international exchange of developmental research. Neither membership in the Society nor affiliation with the academic discipline of psychology is relevant in considering a *Monographs* submission.

The corresponding author for any manuscript must, in the submission letter, warrant that all coauthors are in agreement with the content of the manuscript. The corresponding author also is responsible for informing all coauthors, in a timely manner, of manuscript submission, editorial decisions, reviews received, and any revisions recommended. Before publication, the corresponding author also must warrant in the submission letter that the study has been conducted according to the ethical guidelines of the Society for Research in Child Development.

Potential authors who may be unsure whether the manuscript they are planning would make an appropriate submission are invited to draft an outline of what they propose, and send it to the Editor for assessment. This mechanism, as well as a more detailed description of all editorial policies, evaluation processes, and format requirements, can be found at the Editorial Office web site (http://astro.temple.edu/~overton/monosrcd.html) or by contacting the Editor, Willis F. Overton, Temple University–Psychology, 1701 North 13th St.—Rm. 567, Philadelphia, PA 19122-6085 (e-mail: monosrcd@blue.vm.temple.edu) (telephone: 1-215-204-7718).

Monographs of the Society for Research in Child Development (ISSN 0037-976X), one of three publications of the Society for Research in Child Development, is published four times a year by Blackwell Publishers, Inc., with offices at 350 Main Street, Malden, MA 02148, USA, and 108 Cowley Road, Oxford OX4 1JF, UK. Call US 1-800-835-6770, fax: (781) 388-8232, or e-mail: subscrip@ blackwellpub.com. A subscription to *Monographs of the SRCD* comes with a subscription to *Child Development* (published six times a year in February, April, June, August, October, and December). A combined package rate is also available with the third SRCD publication, *Child Development Abstracts and Bibliography*, published three times a year.

INFORMATION FOR SUBSCRIBERS   For new orders, renewals, sample copy requests, claims, change of address, and all other subscription correspondence, please contact the Journals Subscription Department at the publisher's Malden office.

INSTITUTIONAL SUBSCRIPTION RATES FOR MONOGRAPHS OF THE SRCD/CHILD DEVELOPMENT 2001   The Americas $293, Rest of World £192. All orders must be paid by credit card, business check, or money order. Checks and money orders should be made payable to Blackwell Publishers. Canadian residents please add 7% GST.

INSTITUTIONAL SUBSCRIPTION RATES FOR MONOGRAPHS OF THE SRCD/CHILD DEVELOPMENT/CHILD DEVELOPMENT ABSTRACTS AND BIBLIOGRAPHY 2001   The Americas $369, Rest of World £246. All orders must be paid by credit card, business check, or money order. Checks and money orders should be made payable to Blackwell Publishers. Canadian residents please add 7% GST.

BACK ISSUES   Back issues are available from the publisher's Malden office.

MICROFORM   The journal is available on microfilm. For microfilm service, address inquiries to Bell and Howell Information and Learning, 300 North Zeeb Road, Ann Arbor, MI 48106-1346, USA. Bell and Howell Serials Customer Service Department: 1-800-521-0600 ×2873.

POSTMASTER   Periodicals class postage paid at Boston, MA, and additional offices. Send address changes to Blackwell Publishers, 350 Main Street, Malden, MA 02148, USA.

CURRENT